Essentials of Business Processes and Information Systems

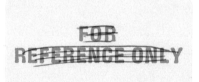

Essentials of Business Processes and Information Systems

Simha R. Magal, PhD
Grand Valley State University

Jeffrey Word
Manchester Business School and SAP AG

WILEY

JOHN WILEY & SONS, INC.

WRITTEN WITH THE SUPPORT OF

VP & Executive Publisher   *Don Fowley*
Executive Editor   *Beth Lang Golub*
Senior Production Editor   *Nicole Repasky*
Marketing Manager   *Christopher Ruel*
Designer   *Jim O'Shea*
Production Management Services   *Pine Tree Composition, Inc.*
Media Editor   *Lauren Sapira*
Cover Photo   *AAGAMIA/Getty Images*

This book was set in Times Roman by Laserwords Private Limited and printed and bound by Hamilton Printing. The cover was printed by Hamilton Printing.

This book is printed on acid-free paper. ♾

To order books or for customer service please, call 1-800-CALL WILEY (225-5945).

Library of Congress Cataloging-in-Publication Data
Magal, Simha R.
    Essentials of business processes and informtion systems / Simha R. Magal, Jeffrey Word.
        p. cm.
Includes index.
ISBN 978-0-470-23059-6 (pbk.)
1. Management information systems. 2. Business planning–Data Processing. I. Word, Jeffrey. II. Title.

HD30.213.M333   2009
658.4'038011–dc22

                                    2008042918

Printed in the United States of America

10 9 8

Preface

As more and more businesses adopt enterprise systems globally, it becomes increasingly important for business schools to offer a more process-centric education to better reflect the realities of the modern business environment. Given the tight integration between business operations and enterprise systems, we have designed *Essentials of Business Processes and Information Systems* to reflect how real-world business processes are managed and executed in a practical and accessible format. Business students, regardless of their functional discipline, will be able to apply the real-world concepts discussed in this text immediately on entering the workforce. We have designed our textbook to be used as a supplement in either an introductory MIS or a general business course to establish a fundamental understanding of business processes and the enterprise systems that enable them.

Essentials of Business Processes and Information Systems deals with the key processes that are common in most companies, and it illustrates how enterprise systems enable companies to execute those processes quickly and efficiently. The objective of this text is to bridge the gap between the fundamentals of how businesses operate (processes) and the tools that business people use to accomplish their tasks (enterprise systems). We have written this book with the assumption that students have only limited experience with business or information systems. We therefore have presented the fundamental concepts in a manner that introductory students will find accessible.

Because the modern business environment is highly complex, we have focused *Essentials of Business Processes and Information Systems* around three generic processes: procurement, fulfillment, and production. We are convinced that this approach will provide students who don't have extensive background information with a clear understanding of how different functional groups inside a company interact to accomplish work. We also use this process-based approach to introduce students to the role of enterprise systems in eliminating inefficiencies and improving performance. We illustrate these discussions with multiple examples from real-world companies.

Essentials of Business Processes and Information Systems uses a blended-learning approach comprised of three unique aspects, in addition to the traditional textbook content: case studies, a two-step learning process, and the simulated SAP® environment.

Case Study. To illustrate the key process and enterprise system concepts, we have integrated a straightforward case throughout the book. The case describes a hypothetical manufacturing organization to present the key flows, data and information, activities, and personnel that characterize a modern business. It also demonstrates how the various functions and processes utilize enterprise systems. Finally, it serves as a basis for student assignments.

A Two-Step Learning Process. Students will first learn the fundamentals of each process on paper—that is, the process flowcharts and physical documents associated with the process—and then execute them in a simulated SAP® environment. This approach highlights the contrasts between traditional paper-based (manual) and modern system-based (automated) process execution.

Simulated SAP® ERP Environment. Students will complete the assignments and exercises in the textbook using the market-leading enterprise software, SAP. We wrote *Essentials of Business Processes and Information Systems* in partnership with SAP and have developed a Web-based system that simulates the use of the most recent version of SAP® ERP software. Although the use of SAP software is incorporated into the text and assignments, the concepts and terminology are applicable to any business and any enterprise system. Note: This book is *not* an SAP training manual. Although the simulated SAP environment is very similar to a real SAP environment, it is highly simplified so that it focuses on process concepts rather than software functionality.

In order to facilitate assigning and tracking of students' completion of the simulations, we are delivering the simulations via WileyPLUS, Wiley's online teaching and learning platform. ***A WileyPLUS registration code is required to access the simulations in WileyPLUS.***

WileyPLUS—INFORMATION FOR PROFESSORS

This textbook can be used with or without the simulation component. To facilitate this, two ordering options are available - one with the WileyPLUS registration code for the simulations and one without. The WileyPLUS registration code is packaged with new books at no extra charge.

To order this textbook with the WileyPLUS registration code, use this ISBN on your bookstore order form: 978-0470-48276-6.
(IF YOU WANT YOUR STUDENTS TO USE THE SAP SIMULATIONS, YOU MUST USE THIS ISBN FOR ORDERING!)

To order this textbook only, with no access to the simulations, use this ISBN: 978-0-470-23059-6.

Before the start of your term, your Wiley Representative or WileyPLUS Account Manager will help you with everything you need to get started. First, they will help you create a unique WileyPLUS URL for your course. You must give this URL to your students in order for them to register for WileyPLUS. Students must go to the URL and register for WileyPLUS using a registration code that will be packaged with the book or available for sale separately online.

For more information on WileyPLUS, please contact your Wiley Representative (www.wiley.com/college/rep) or visit http://www.wileyplus.com.

WileyPLUS—INFORMATION FOR STUDENTS

The SAP simulations and quizzes your professor may be assigning you for this course are available in WileyPLUS, an online teaching and learning platform. In order for you to access these assignments, you must use WileyPLUS.

If your professor ordered a registration code packaged with the text AND *if you purchased a new textbook* from your bookstore, you will have received a WileyPLUS registration code packaged with this textbook.

At the start of your course, your professor will give you a WileyPLUS URL. To complete your assignments, you must first go to this URL and register. At the URL, click the "Register" button, and walk through the process of creating your account. At the appropriate point in the process, you will enter the registration code that came packaged with this textbook.

If you purchased a used textbook, you must purchase a registration code separately. Students may purchase registration codes online using a credit card. First, you must go to the WileyPLUS URL provided by your instructor. At the URL, click on the "Register" button, and walk through the process of creating your account. When you reach the screen that prompts you to enter a registration code, you can link directly to the product you need and purchase it with a credit card.

For more information, talk with your professor or visit www.wileyplus.com.

FEEDBACK

The authors and publisher invite students and instructors to ask questions, make comments, and communicate directly with the BP&IS team on the following Web site: ***www.extrabandwidth.com/forum***

Acknowledgments

The authors and publisher wish to acknowledge the contribution of the following individuals for their assistance in preparing and reviewing this textbook.

The many faculty and students in the Seidman College of Business, who have helped evolve the concept of this book over the years. We particularly wish to acknowledge the contributions of Helen Klein with whom one of the authors has had many discussions about how best to teach about processes, and Robert Garst, David Herrema, and Eric Koch, who helped tremendously. We are very grateful to Nina Simosko and Don Bulmer for their executive support for this book at SAP.

We are also very grateful to the efforts of Robert Weiss, who tirelessly reviewed and edited our work and provided invaluable guidance in improving it. We wish to thank the reviewers, Cynthia Barnes, Lamar University; Traci Carte, Oklahoma University; Don Chand, Bentley College; Paul Cheney, University of Central Florida; Stylianos Drakatos, Florida International University; Lauren Eder, Rider University; Donna Everett, Morehead State University; Soundararajan Ezekiel, Indiana University of Pennsylvania; Steve Hunt, Morehead State University; Hassan Ibrahim, University of Maryland; Shin-jeng Lin, LeMoyne College; Bill MacKinnon, Clarkson University; Purnendu Mandal, Lamar University; Earl McKinney, Bowling Green State University; Sue Pfeifer, Valley City State University; Farnaz Sharifrazi, National University; Catherine Usoff, Bentley College; B. S. Vijayaraman, University of Akron; and Tom Wilder, CSU Chico, for reviewing the book. Finally, we wish to recognize the efforts of Beth Lang Golub and her colleagues at Wiley for keeping us moving and getting this book written.

The case study (Super Skateboard Builders, Inc (SSB)) and the various exercises and assignments included in this book are based on the efforts of several faculty members in the Seidman College of Business, Grand Valley State University, that were funded by grants by the Seidman College of Business. We acknowledge efforts of the Seidman faculty and are grateful to the Seidman College for granting us permission to use the case and data in this book.

We also acknowledge the support from the Fred Meijer Center for Writing at Grand Valley State University in completing this book.

Writing a book can be stressful at times, especially for the authors' families. Our families' patience and encouragement while writing this book has been invaluable. The authors and publisher gratefully acknowledge SAP's kind permission to use its trademarks in this publication. SAP AG is not the publisher of this book and is not responsible for it under any aspect of press law.

Author Biographies

Simha R. Magal, PhD, is professor of management (MIS) and director, ERP initiative, in the Seidman College of Business, Grand Valley State University. He received his PhD from the University of Georgia. His primary research interests include e-business and enterprise systems. His articles have appeared in such publications as *MIS Quarterly, Journal of MIS*, and *Information and Management*, among others. He is editor of AISWorld Net (www.aisworld.org) and has served on the editorial boards of several journals. He served as cochair of the inaugural conference of the Midwest Association for Information Systems (MWAIS) in 2006 and as president of MWAIS during 2008–2009.

Jeff Word is vice president of product strategy, SAP AG. Mr. Word is responsible for defining SAP's future product strategy and fostering product innovation inside SAP. For more than 14 years, Mr. Word has worked for Global 1000 companies in the high-tech industry, specializing in business consulting and IT strategy. At SAP he has driven the evolution of enterprise technology strategy with a special focus on corporate process improvement initiatives and services-based IT architecture design.

Mr. Word is currently completing a doctorate in information systems at Manchester Business School in England. His research focus is on event-driven process design and next-generation enterprise architecture. He earned an MBA in international management from the Thunderbird School of Global Management (1999). He also earned a BA in European studies and Spanish from the University of Oklahoma (1994).

Brief Contents

Business Processes in Practice

Contents

CHAPTER 1

Organizations, Business Processes, and Information Systems

Learning Objectives

After completing this chapter, you should be able to:

▶ Understand that work in organizations is completed in processes that consist of many steps.

▶ Compare and contrast the functional and process views of organizations and identify the negative consequences of the traditional functional organizational structure.

▶ Discuss and describe the various flows in a process — physical, data, document, and information.

▶ Explain how enterprise systems enable organizations to execute and manage processes.

Based on the fact that you are taking a college or university course that uses this book as part of the curriculum, it is safe to assume that you are planning some sort of career in business. You might be considering a career in marketing, finance, or accounting, or you might even start your own business. Alternatively, you might not have any idea of what you want to be when you "grow up," and this course sounded like something that would be a good introduction to business — "just in case." Either way, you are probably wondering what *business processes* are and why they are important enough for your instructor to include them in this course. You also might be curious regarding the types of *information and communication technology* (ICT) that companies use to run their businesses. Briefly, business processes are the tasks or activities that companies use to produce goods or services, and these activities are increasingly supported by ICT, such as computers, the Internet, the Web, and, *information systems*.

We will examine business processes and ICT more closely later in the chapter and then address them throughout this book. Before you start learning about them in detail, however, it will help if you understand why they are critical to modern business operations. Thus, we begin this chapter by discussing the global competitive environment in which contemporary organizations operate. The need to compete in this environment has led organizations to increasingly view their operations in terms of business processes and to develop information systems to support these processes.

We then define and discuss business processes, information systems, and their role in modern organizations in more detail. Finally, we develop a framework that we will use in later chapters to increase your understanding of business processes, the role of information systems in supporting these processes, and the financial impact of business processes on organizations.

As illustrated in the boxed feature, Business Processes in Practice 1-1, the challenges presented by globalization have a huge impact on companies' business and information technology (IT) strategies. To effectively adapt to the changing global environment of the technology industry, Apple needed to adopt a process view of their business and to implement information technology systems to support those processes.

▶ 1.1 THE MODERN GLOBAL BUSINESS ENVIRONMENT

The Apple case illustrates the competitive environment to which modern organizations must adapt. To fully understand the modern business world, you need to become familiar with the terms *"global competition," "information revolution,"* and *"knowledge worker."* What exactly do these terms mean, and why do they appear at the beginning of an introductory book on business processes? Finally—and perhaps most important—why should they matter to you?

As we discuss in this section, we introduce these three concepts because they are likely to have a major impact on the world of business in the foreseeable future. Thus, it is very important that you understand them in order to develop a "big picture" of the business environment in which your future employers will be operating.

1.1.1 Global Competition

Evidence that we live in a **global competitive environment** is all around us. We see it, for example, in the products and services we use. Rarely will you find a product that is designed and produced entirely in one country. More often, the product is designed in one country, the parts to make the product are produced in several countries, the product is assembled in another country, and service and support for the product are provided by people in yet another country.

Why has this shift toward globalization occurred? There are clearly many reasons, including national and international politics and policies. Regardless of the reasons, however, the fact remains that over the last several years, organizations have relocated parts of their operations to places outside their home countries to take advantage of unique business efficiencies. For example, companies have moved manufacturing to places where labor is less expensive, and they have transferred research and development to locations that offer an abundant supply of highly educated scientists and engineers.

As you see in Business Processes in Practice 1-1 Apple designs its products in California, but it produces them in specialized contract manufacturing facilities in Asia. These contract manufacturers are not owned by Apple; in fact, they often produce products for Apple's competitors in the same facilities. Because these manufacturers are so specialized in producing electronic products, they can fabricate very high quality finished goods at a lower cost than Apple could in its own factories. Apple can then invest the money it saves by outsourcing its production process in hiring more researchers and designers in California.

Another type of relocation of processes and operations actually results in new factories and production facilities being built in the United States. For many years,

► *BUSINESS PROCESSES IN PRACTICE 1-1*

APPLE COMPUTERS

Apple Computers (now Apple Inc.) is a good example of a company that has embraced globalization and has grown very quickly by taking advantage of integrated business processes and information technology. If you have ever purchased or used an Apple iPod, you probably have noticed a label on the back that reads, "Designed by Apple in California, Assembled in China." Apple does not manufacture iPods in its own factories. In fact, it hardly has any factories anymore.

In 1998, Apple Computer was a much different company than it is today. For one thing, there weren't any iPods or iPhones or Apple Stores. The company sold only Mac laptop and desktop computers and a few other similar products. In fact, Apple produced only six main products and sold them almost entirely through a network of resellers. The company manufactured these products in their main factories in Ireland and Singapore, and they controlled every aspect of production and distribution, from the initial design through the delivery of finished products to their resellers. Apple's resellers were typically small, specialized local computer firms that placed orders with Apple for computers and then sold them to local companies or individuals. Unless you knew exactly where to look, it was often difficult to find an Apple computer. In addition, Apple had very little knowledge about its customers because the resellers, and not Apple, actually sold the computers to them.

Over the next 10 years, Apple Computers evolved into Apple Inc., a much larger and more visible company. Consider these numbers. In 1998, Apple Computers had 6,658 employees and less than $6 billion in revenues. At the beginning of 2008, Apple Inc. had 21,600 employees and more than $24 billion in revenues. In 1998, Apple generated almost all its revenues through reseller channels. By 2008 they had opened nearly 200 retail stores all over the world and had nearly $4 billion in revenues just from those stores and Internet sales. Apple's product line had also grown from 6 to more than 27 main products, including digital music, movies, and television through iTunes.

How and why did this transformation occur? The answer is that several things occurred in 1998 that signaled this rapid growth and expansion for Apple and resulted in some major changes in the way the company operated. First, Steve Jobs returned to Apple as its CEO after several years outside the company. At the time Jobs returned, Apple wasn't doing very well. In an attempt to turn the company around, Jobs instituted some very big and difficult changes. Jobs understood that Apple needed to focus on its core competency: designing easy-to-use and engaging hardware and software products. He immediately revamped the product line by modernizing the Mac operating system and providing Apple computers with new Internet capabilities.

In addition, Jobs started to outsource manufacturing operations to specialized high-tech manufacturing companies, primarily located in Asia. Because Apple's core competency was designing the products, they did not need to continue to manufacture these products themselves. Jobs's next initiative was to launch the Apple Online Store to sell products directly to consumers over the Internet. Getting close to customers was crucial for Apple's plans to provide users with a better and more engaging experience. Finally, Jobs implemented SAP R/3, an enterprise system, to manage all the new processes that resulted from the other strategic changes in product design, manufacturing, and sales.

Every one of the strategic business changes that Apple made in 1998 fundamentally transformed the core business processes that had been in place for many years. For these new processes to be effective, they had to be visible and accessible to employees across Apple's entire spectrum of business operations. They also had to eliminate several areas of inefficiency among groups in the company. The information systems that were in place in 1998 could not grow to support the expansion in product categories, geographic locations, and revenues. Therefore, Apple had to implement an integrated enterprise system that would be able to grow flexibly as the company's business expanded.

Since 1998 Apple has continuously expanded its enterprise system to incorporate new business processes and capabilities. By 2008 Apple had one of the largest and most advanced integrated enterprise systems in the world. The company manages every iPod, iPhone, Mac, and other Apple product from the design phase through final sales in a set of integrated enterprise systems. In fact, Apple's enterprise systems are so critical that its business would come to a halt if these systems stopped working for even a few minutes.

Source: Compiled from Apple Inc. Annual Reports; and "Hard Sell," *Information Week*, March 1, 1999.

Toyota designed and built its automobiles in Japan and then shipped them to the United States to be sold. After analyzing the costs and benefits, Toyota realized that if they could build a production facility in the United States and ensure that it would maintain the same high-quality production processes as their plants in Japan, they would save a significant amount of money that they could then reinvest in new product design back in Japan.

One consequence of globalization is increased competition. Companies are no longer limited to their local markets. Instead, the world is their market. Of course, as a company's market expands, so do the number and types of firms with which it competes. This increased global competition puts pressure on companies to be more efficient and productive. In addition, they must develop strategies to tightly integrate their operations, which can be distributed across many different geographic locations. Clearly, then, globalization has significant implications for how organizations operate. This observation brings us to the second term mentioned in the opening paragraph—information revolution.

1.1.2 The Information Revolution

Information revolution refers to the increased use of information and communication technology to create, deliver, and use information. ICT includes such things as the Internet (e.g., e-mail, Web) and computer-based business information systems (e.g., SAP® ERP) that support the work of organizations. The information revolution plays an important role in the global competitive environment. As we saw, because organizations are expanding and their processes are becoming widely dispersed, it is vital that they exchange and share information efficiently and accurately. ICT has helped organizations to globalize their operations by enabling them to coordinate business processes that are performed around the world.

If we look back at the Apple and Toyota examples, both of those companies use very advanced ICT capabilities to manage their distributed operations and partner networks. For example, Apple must quickly communicate any changes in its sales forecasts to its Asian contract manufacturers to ensure that they can adjust their production capacities to meet the new sales requirements. Toyota must closely monitor every aspect of its production facilities to ensure that the quality of cars and trucks manufactured in the United States meets the same standards as those manufactured in Japan.

The only way for Apple and Toyota to effectively monitor, manage, and communicate between their distributed networks of facilities and partners is to utilize ICT effectively. They simply could not control such complicated and intertwined global processes without the aid of ICT.

Significantly, the ability to communicate instantly via documents, data voice, and video makes it unnecessary for everybody involved in designing and producing a product to be in the same location. In this sense, then, ICT enables, supports, and even encourages globalization. At the same time, however, organizations are becoming critically dependent on ICT to run smoothly, precisely because their various operations are spread all over the world. In addition, they rely on ICT to be more productive and thus remain competitive. The danger here is that, if the ICT doesn't function properly, the entire organization can't function.

Clearly, then, people in modern organizations increasingly depend on information to do their work. For this reason these employees are increasingly referred to as knowledge workers based on the large amount of decisions they must make and the information they must constantly analyze.

1.1.3 The Knowledge Worker

A **knowledge worker** is one who uses ICT to create, acquire, process, synthesize, disseminate, analyze, and use information to be more productive. Examples of knowledge workers are product manager, sales executive, production manager, and financial analyst. Knowledge workers perform work that often requires both *structured information* and *unstructured information* from multiple sources. Structured information is well defined, and its source is known; that is, a manager will know what information is needed and where to find it. Unstructured information is not well defined or readily available; that is, a manager may not know what information is needed or where to find it.

Knowledge work is typically nonroutine in that it is not repeated throughout the course of the workday or workweek. For example, product managers might speak to customers on a monthly basis to collect feedback regarding their products. Although they may do this in regular meetings, this work is not considered routine because each interaction with the customer is very different. For example, one meeting might deal with a quality issue related to a particular product, whereas another meeting might focus on a new feature that was added to the product. To perform these tasks successfully, knowledge workers must have a thorough understanding of the business processes that occur across different areas of the company. They also must be able to work with multifunctional teams from different groups.

In contrast to knowledge workers, *task workers* perform routine, structured tasks, typically in a repeated manner. Task workers include customer service representatives, purchasing and accounting clerks, and insurance claims processors. Task workers are usually confined to one specific set of tasks in their functional area and are required to deal with other areas of the company only in rare cases. Although task workers are extremely important to the operations of the company, they tend to have a much more narrow view of the overall business, and compared to knowledge workers, they use information in a much more specific way.

Knowledge workers are employed in all parts of an organization, not just in IT departments. *In all likelihood, you will be a knowledge worker at some point in your career.* As a knowledge worker, you must develop the skills to find and use the information you need rather than rely on others to find it for you. As one company executive recently remarked: "We have technology coming out of our ears, but not enough people who know how to use it." In other words, his organization does not have enough knowledge workers.

To be an effective knowledge worker, you must understand how, where, and why the underlying data are generated. Significantly, the data that are essential to your work are frequently generated by your coworkers, just as the data you create affect others. In other words, you must understand the "big picture" of your organization and not just your part in it. For example, a product manager must deal extensively with the detailed customer data forwarded by the sales group and reconcile these data with the product features coming from the design group and the production data generated by the operations group

What does all this have to do with your decision to take what might be your first course in business? The answer is that we want to impress on you the importance of some key skills that companies are desperately looking for in a good knowledge worker:

1. **Strategic Thinking.** The ability to see the big picture and understand how your organization works as a whole.

2. **Information Literacy.** The ability to determine what information is needed, where to find it, and how to use it.

3. **Communication and Collaboration.** The ability to function as an effective part of a project team where you understand your role as well as the roles of others.

You will develop these skills during your tenure in college and refine them as you gain experience in the workplace. However, you need a solid foundation on which to build. This foundation is a thorough understanding of both the fundamental business processes that organizations use to do their work and the role ICT plays in supporting these processes. In the next section, we take a closer look at some of these fundamental processes.

1.1.4 Key Business Processes

Organizations create and deliver value in the form of a product or service, which they offer to consumers or to other organizations. Manufacturing organizations create tangible products such as cars, flashlights, and skateboards. Other organizations create intangible "products" or services such as education, health, information, and financial services. Regardless of the type of organization, however, the product or service is created via a sequence of tasks or activities that take a set of inputs and convert them into the desired output. We refer to this sequence of activities as a **business process**. Figure 1.1 illustrates a process in its most basic, or generic, form. A process consists of multiple sequential *steps* or *activities* that produce some outcome or output.

Organizations today use a number of processes. However, most of our discussions will focus on three fundamental processes: procurement, production, and fulfillment. In the **procurement process**, the organization acquires the basic materials that it uses to produce goods or services. The **production process**, as its name implies, involves manufacturing or generating the desired goods and services. Finally, in the **fulfillment process**, the company delivers the goods or services to its customers or resellers.

We have included these three processes in this book because they are typically considered the "core" processes that exist in most companies. Going further, we describe each process in simple terms to provide a big picture of how it works. In reality, these processes are far more complex, and they differ greatly among companies and industries. Because this is an introductory text, it is not terribly important that you understand every variation and difference between processes in every industry. Rather, our goal is to communicate the basic concepts and vocabulary of these core processes so that you can quickly adapt this knowledge to the company and industry where you will eventually start your career.

To understand how modern organizations utilize these processes, let's use the example of a company that manufactures skateboards. This company takes

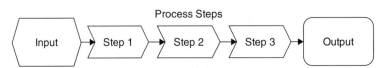

Figure 1.1   Generic process

Figure 1.2 Procurement process

the different components (input)—such as a board, wheels, nuts, and bolts—and assembles them into a skateboard. It then inspects the skateboard for quality and packs it in a box. Assembly, inspection, and packing are the required steps or activities. The result (output) is skateboards. Because the objective of these activities is to produce or manufacture the skateboard, this sequence of activities constitutes the production process.

Before the company undertakes the production process, however, it must first acquire the necessary components, or raw materials. This is the procurement process. This process might include the steps shown in Figure 1.2. First, someone in the company determines how many of which materials are needed, by whom, and by which date. He or she then completes a purchase requisition for these materials. The next steps are to select a suitable supplier and to create and send a purchase order to the supplier. The supplier then ships the materials, which the company receives and stores in its warehouse. The supplier also sends an invoice, which the company pays. Thus, the result or outcome of the procurement process is an inventory of materials in stock.

The third key process—the fulfillment process—generally occurs after the company has completed the production process. The fulfillment process is concerned with filling a customer order, and it might include the five steps shown in Figure 1.3. First, the organization receives a customer's order over the phone. It then prepares and ships the order to the customer, along with an invoice. Finally, the customer sends a payment to the company.

The skateboard company we just discussed manufactures its own product. Now, let's consider an organization that buys and sells products but does not actually make them. That is, the organization buys finished products from a supplier, stores them in a warehouse, and fills customer orders from this inventory.

A familiar example of such a company is Amazon.com. Amazon purchases books from publishers such as John Wiley & Sons (procurement), puts those books in its warehouses, and then ships them to customers when they place an order on the Web site (fulfillment). Amazon.com does not manufacture any books (production); it simply resells books from other companies. This is a very efficient business model for Amazon because it can sell an almost infinite number of books from many publishers on its Web site, and it does not have to worry about dealing with the authors, editors, bookbinders, paper manufacturers, and ink suppliers involved with producing the actual books.

Figure 1.3 Fulfillment process

In contrast to the skateboard manufacturer, then, Amazon.com has no production process. Therefore, it has only two key processes: procurement and fulfillment. Amazon's procurement process differs somewhat from that for the skateboard manufacturer because Amazon doesn't make its products. Therefore, instead of purchasing raw materials (e.g., paper and ink), it acquires the final products (books).

These examples are deliberately very simplistic. There are many details and additional steps associated with these processes, which we will discuss in later chapters. For now, it's sufficient to understand the basic activities involved in the three processes.

It is very important, however, to recognize that the activities involved in processes are carried out by individuals located in different parts of the organization. Most companies group their employees into different units. The manner in which they group their people is determined by the organization's structure and design, and it has significant implications for how well the various processes are executed.

▶ 1.2 THE FUNCTIONAL ORGANIZATIONAL STRUCTURE

The most common organizational structure is the **functional structure**. Organizations that utilize a functional structure are divided into *functions*, or departments, each of which is responsible for a set of closely related activities. For example, the accounting department sends and receives payments, and the warehouse receives and ships goods and materials. Typical functions or departments found in a modern organization include *purchasing, operations, warehouse (inventory management), sales and marketing, research and development, finance and accounting, human resources*, and *information technology*. Figure 1.4 identifies the key functions, and Table 1-1 describes the basic activities that each function performs.

Go back to the procurement and fulfillment processes that we introduced earlier, and think for a minute about where in the organization the various activities are performed or who in the organization is responsible for performing them. (To keep things simple, we won't deal with production in this chapter.) We'll begin with procurement. In this process, the warehouse determines what it needs, and it creates the purchase requisition. The purchasing department then selects the supplier and creates and sends the purchase order to the supplier. The warehouse receives the goods from the supplier and places them into inventory. Finally, the accounting department receives the invoice from the supplier and makes the payment. For the fulfillment process, the sales department takes the order, the warehouse packs and ships the order, and the accounting department sends the invoice and receives payment.

Figure 1.4 Functional organization

TABLE 1-1   Basic Activities in a Functional Organizational Structure

Functions	Key Activities
Purchasing	Identify vendors Select vendors Create and send purchase orders to vendors Evaluate vendor performance
Warehouse (Inventory Management)	Receive goods from vendors Perform quality inspection of goods received Prepare goods to be returned to vendors Prepare goods for shipment to customers Ship goods to customers Receive goods returned by customers
Operations	Plan capacity Design workflow Schedule production Execute production Perform quality inspection of goods produced
Marketing and Sales	Identify customers Manage relationships with customers Promote products and services Receive customer orders Initiate processing of customer orders Provide after-sales service
Research and Development	Conduct research Develop/refine products Develop/refine processes
Finance and Accounting	Process incoming payments from customers Process outgoing payments to vendors Manage cash flow Manage capital needs Prepare financial statements
Human Resources	Identify workforce needs Recruit employees Hire employees Train employees Evaluate (appraise) employees Manage compensation Manage employee rights and benefits
Information Systems	Help process transactions Capture transaction data Provide information to monitor processes Provide information to detect and define problems with processes Provide information and tools to solve problems

Clearly, then, the procurement and fulfillment processes consist of activities that occur in different, seemingly unrelated functions or departments. In other words, these processes are *cross-functional*; no single group or function is responsible for their execution. For the process to be successfully completed, then, the company must rely on each functional group to execute its individual steps in the process.

If value in organizations is created by processes such as procurement and fulfillment, why, then, are organizations structured according to function? Shouldn't they be structured according to processes? Wouldn't it make sense to group people who deal with all the steps in a process into one unit?

To answer these questions, we need to briefly examine the history of organizations in the United States. Since the beginning of the 20th century, the United States has experienced tremendous growth in organizations. As the organizations grew larger, they also became more complex and difficult to manage. In smaller organizations, managers can typically see what is happening fairly easily—there are few people involved, and they are typically located in one place. One person can manage all the people involved very effectively. If the manager wants to know what is happening in sales, he can talk with one of the few salespeople. If he wants to see how many finished goods are available in inventory, he can examine the warehouse shelves. If he wants to know how production is going, he can walk down and talk to the factory workers.

As companies grow, however, it becomes increasingly difficult to physically monitor all these activities and manage all the people involved because these activities involve a much greater number of employees spread across multiple geographical areas. Eventually, a company can grow to a size at which it becomes impossible to manage processes effectively and to remain competitive without distributing this responsibility to specialized groups.

The need to simplify and better manage activities led organizations to adopt the functional structure. This structure involves the principles of division of labor and specialization. Grouping people who perform similar tasks or functions into one department or unit made it easier to manage the people and the activities they perform. It also allowed groups—or teams—to perform one activity extremely well by isolating each team from the distractions of other groups.

By design, a functional structure is a *bureaucracy* that includes administrative rules and procedures intended to help manage large organizations. The functional organization persists today; in fact, most large organizations are structured by function. The university or college where you are studying right now very likely mirrors the functional organization found in most companies. Inside the business school, there is an accounting department, finance department, marketing department, operations department, and so on.

1.2.1 The Silo Effect

The functional structure served organizations well for a number of years because it enabled them to cope with the challenges generated by their rapid growth. Over time, however, this system developed a serious drawback. Put simply, people in the different functional areas came to perform their steps in the process in isolation, without fully understanding what steps happen before and what steps happen next. They essentially complete their part of the process, hand it off to the next person, and then proceed to the next task. By focusing so narrowly on their specific tasks, they lose sight of the "big picture" of the larger process, be it procurement, fulfillment, or anything else. This tendency is commonly referred to as the **silo effect** because workers complete their tasks in their functional ''silos'' without regard to the consequences for the other components of the process.

A key point here is that the silo nature of the functional organizational structure and the cross-functional nature of processes are at odds with each other. That is, while workers focus on their specific function, each business process involves workers located in multiple functions. A major challenge facing organizations, then, is to effectively coordinate the activities among the different functions or departments. For example, in the procurement process, how does the person in the warehouse who is requisitioning the product inform the purchasing department of the need? How does the receiver in the warehouse know which order just came in? How does the accountant know what the invoice he just received is for and whether it should it be paid? In the fulfillment process, how does the salesperson communicate the customer order to the other employees involved in the process? How does the warehouse know that a customer order has been received and authorized for delivery? When does the accountant send the invoice? Unless the organization carefully coordinates the activities taking place in different functions, it cannot execute the process.

How does an organization achieve this type of coordination? The key is to exchange information efficiently and effectively. People in each step in a process must be informed when it is time for them to complete their step. This exchange of information takes place in a number of ways. In a manual environment, companies use paper documents to communicate information among different departments. In the case of the fulfillment process, for instance, the salesperson completes a multipart sales order document, keeps one part, and sends the remaining parts of the document to the warehouse. The shipper in the warehouse updates the document to reflect her work, keeps a copy, and sends the remaining parts to the accounting department. This process includes many opportunities for error. For example, what happens if the salesperson forgets to send the paperwork to the warehouse? What if the warehouse ships the goods to the customer but forgets to send the paperwork to the accountant? What if the paperwork gets lost? These examples illustrate the importance of coordination in executing processes. Unfortunately, in many organizations, the coordination of work across the process is not very efficient, is time consuming, and results in numerous problems: delays, excess inventory, and lack of visibility across the process. Let's take a closer look at each of these problems.

1.2.2 Delays in Executing the Process

The first consequence of poor coordination is *delays* caused by the time it takes to communicate information among different parts of the process. When an organization performs this coordination manually—for example, by using the multipart sales order document in our fulfillment process—delays are inevitable. Further, requiring employees to complete, forward, and file paperwork wastes time that they could be devoting to their tasks. Finally, in addition to causing delays, this paperwork constitutes a significant cost incurred by the company. Figure 1.5 illustrates the two sources of delays in the fulfillment process: delays due to the need to maintain paperwork and delays in sending the paperwork to other functions.

Delays occur in the form of increased *lead times* (e.g., how far in advance a company must plan to obtain raw materials from its suppliers) and *cycle times* (i.e., the amount of time needed to produce a product or process a customer order). Increased lead times can cause a company to have an insufficient inventory of material when it is needed. Increased cycle times can prevent the company from producing goods and filling customer orders in a timely manner. Both of these

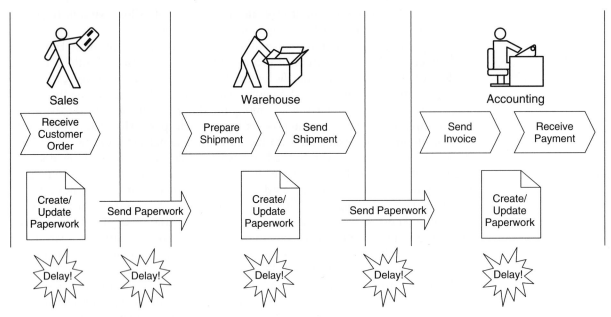

Figure 1.5 A paper-based process

problems can lead to lost sales, as the case of Nintendo Wii illustrates (see Business Processes in Practice 1-2).

1.2.3 Excess Inventory

The second consequence of poor coordination among functions is *excess inventory*. Companies that are plagued by delays and poor communication frequently tend to "cover themselves" by creating a buffer of inventory. Thus, the factory manager will keep a little extra raw material on hand, just in case the purchasing

---

▶ **BUSINESS PROCESSES IN PRACTICE 1-2**

NINTENDO WII

When Nintendo introduced the Wii gaming console in 2007, it was an immediate hit with consumers. In fact, it became so popular so quickly that Nintendo was unable to build enough units to keep up with the demand. The company had sufficient production capacity, but their factories weren't building enough units because they couldn't get the necessary amounts of raw materials from their suppliers as quickly as they needed them. Nintendo had planned for the manufacturing capacity to meet demand, but it had failed to communicate the increased requirements to both their purchasing department and their raw material suppliers.

The increased lead times for raw materials in turn led to a severe increase in the cycle times for production

and delivery of finished goods to stores. That is, it took Nintendo much longer to produce the Wii because the factories had to wait for suppliers to provide them with the necessary materials. As a result, Nintendo missed an opportunity to sell more products and meet the consumer demand. These delays not only cost Nintendo a great deal of revenue, but they also enabled Nintendo's competitors to sell their products to consumers who otherwise would have purchased the Wii. One analyst estimated that the Wii shortage cost Nintendo close to US$1.3 billion.

Source: Compiled from Nintendo company reports; and "A Year Later, the Same Scene: Long Lines for the Elusive Wii," *New York Times*, December 14, 2007.

▶ *BUSINESS PROCESSES IN PRACTICE 1-3*

CISCO SYSTEMS

In 2001, Cisco Systems was selling huge amounts of their key networking products, driven largely by the dot-com boom. Cisco was having a difficult time keeping up with the demand for their products due to severe shortages of raw materials, so they had placed double and triple orders for some parts with their suppliers to "lock up" the parts. In addition, they had accumulated a "safety stock" of finished goods based on optimistic sales forecasts. When the Internet boom started to crash, however, orders began to taper off quickly. Even more damaging for Cisco, the company was unable to communicate the drop in demand through their organization so that they could reduce their production capacity to sell off their "safety stock" of finished goods and also reduce the amount of raw materials they were purchasing to reduce their supply buffer.

This mismatch between lower demand, substantial inventories of raw materials, and excessive production capacity ultimately forced Cisco to write off more than $2.5 billion of excess inventory from their books in 2001—the largest inventory write-off in history.

Source: Compiled from: Cisco company reports; and "Cisco 'Fesses Up to Bad News," *Infoworld*. April 16, 2001.

process is delayed (which history has shown is often the case), the warehouse manager will stockpile a little extra inventory of raw material and finished goods, just in case the purchasing process and the production process are delayed, and so on. If all the groups involved in the process pile up extra inventory, the result will be an excessive—and costly—amount of extra "just in case" inventory for the organization. The case of Cisco Systems illustrates this process (see Business Processes in Practice 1-3).

1.2.4 Lack of Visibility across Processes

A third consequence of poor coordination is a lack of *visibility across the process*. That is, the people involved in the process do not have information about (1) the status of the process in other parts of the organization and/or (2) how well the process is performing over time. Typically, the paperwork and information about process steps are not readily available to people in other departments. Referring back to Figure 1.5, for instance, in the fulfillment process, once the salesperson sends the customer order to the warehouse, the salesperson receives no follow-up information regarding the subsequent steps in the process. As a result, if the customer calls to inquire about the status of the order, the salesperson has to call the warehouse or the accounting department to track down this information. A costly consequence of not having good visibility across the organization is illustrated in the case of Nike (see Business Processes in Practice 1-4). In this case, the problems were caused by a lack of visibility across multiple processes, not just across one process.

The root cause of these three problems is the tendency to view work in terms of functional silos rather than in terms of cross-functional processes. Because the people in each functional area are focused on their own world, they do not easily see how significant the negative consequences of the little delays, small mistakes, and excess inventory can be to the process or to the organization as a whole. At the process level, small delays can accumulate to significantly extend the time required to fill a customer order or acquire raw materials. Similarly, at the organizational level, small quantities of extra inventory can add up to cost the organization significant amounts of money in terms of storage and opportunity costs.

NIKE

In 2000, Nike produced too many of the wrong shoes and not enough of the right shoes due to a mismatch between what their demand planning process was telling them to produce and what their customers were telling them they wanted. The production planning department generated an incorrect demand forecast within their departmental information system for the shoe group. Compounding this error, the manufacturing, procurement and sales departments never checked to see if the forecast matched what their customers were requesting in the sales department. Instead, these departments simply took the demand forecast generated by the planning system and typed it into the manufacturing system, thereby generating the procurement requirements. The information system in the sales department was never double-checked to determine what the actual customer order levels were.

Even though Nike had highly advanced information systems in its forecasting, manufacturing, sales, and procurement departments, the lack of visibility across the entire process, coupled with manual integration across the departmental systems, cost Nike more than $100 million that quarter. In addition, their share price went down 20% the day after they publicly announced the mistake.

Source: Compiled from: Nike company reports; "Supply Chain Debacle," *Internet Week*, March 5, 2001; and "Nike Rebounds: How (and Why) Nike Recovered from Its Supply Chain Disaster," *CIO Magazine*, June 15, 2004.

Organizations have historically accepted these negative consequences of the functional structure. The early benefits of the functional structure—namely, the ability to better manage rapidly growing organizations—outweighed these consequences. Thus, the functional structure remains a common form of organizing. Today, however, global competition is forcing organizations to become more efficient and effective. As a result, organizations are actively seeking to eliminate or reduce the problems of delays, excess inventories, and lack of visibility. To accomplish these goals, organizations must break out of silos and focus on processes. In other words, they need to substitute a *process view* for the traditional functional view. Dell Corporation is a great example of an organization that is designed around a process rather than functional silos (see Business Processes in Practice 1-5).

DELL

Unlike Nike, which implemented a functional system, Dell is organized around a process view of computer sales and manufacturing. Dell largely operates on a business model that builds computers after the company receives an order from a customer, an approach known as make-to-order. The process of building the computer begins as soon as Dell receives the customer order (and usually the payment). This order triggers different steps, including procuring the components, building the computer to exact specifications, shipping the computer, and so on. In contrast, most other computer manufacturers try to forecast what customers will want and then procure the components needed to produce them. They then build the computers in advance and sell from their stock of finished goods.

Because Dell was a new company and did not have a historical functional organization to deal with, they could radically rethink their process for building and selling computers and then build their company around the new process. This process-based production model enabled Dell to become the leader in the personal computer industry and remain much more profitable than their competitors.

Source: Compiled from: Dell company reports; and "Supply Meets Demand at Dell Inc.," *Accenture*, accessed July 22, 2008, http://www.accenture.com/Global/Services/By_Industry/Communications/Access_Newsletter/Article_Index/SupplyComputer.htm.

A process view is a philosophy that emerged in the early 1990s as a result of the increasing complexity and distributed operations that globalization created. So many companies were acquiring companies in other countries and expanding operations globally that they were running into massive inefficiencies and operational issues. The process view of the enterprise gave companies a powerful way to standardize the way they did their work across many countries and gain significant cost savings as a result.

Because processes span multiple departments across companies—and in many cases across multiple countries—it is not possible to manage these processes manually; that is, using paperwork. For this reason, ICT is an essential part of the process view of organizations. In particular, a class of ICT, known as enterprise systems (ES) or enterprise resource planning (ERP) systems, is essential to managing business processes. At the same time as the process view came into popularity, software companies such as SAP introduced the first integrated enterprise systems. It was the combination of a process view of the company and the capabilities of enterprise systems to manage global processes that brought about a huge shift in the productivity and profitability of many global companies. In today's business reality, the process view and ICT cannot be separated. In the next section, we will discuss the role of information and information systems in supporting business processes.

▶ 1.3 THE IMPORTANCE OF INFORMATION SYSTEMS

Information systems are computer-based systems that capture, store, and retrieve data associated with process activities. In addition, they organize these data into meaningful information that organizations use to support and assess these activities.

1.3.1 Data and Information

Every activity in an organization generates **data**, which are raw facts that, by themselves, have limited value or meaning. Examples of data are customer names, product numbers, and quantities of products sold. By themselves, these facts might not have much value. However, a report that uses these data to summarize product sales over time has tremendous value. Data that are organized in a way that is useful to an organization are referred to as **information**. In this case, the organization can utilize this sales information to determine which products are doing well and which are not.

1.3.2 Functional Information Systems

Although organizations utilize a variety of information systems, most systems—like most organizations—tend to focus on functions rather than processes and are not well integrated. That is, they do not easily share data and information with one another. Once again, this lack of integration arose from historical situations. Systems in organizations have evolved over the years in isolation. That is, each functional area or department developed a system that suited its purposes well. Thus, sales developed order management systems, warehouses developed systems to track inventory of materials, accounting developed systems to track invoices and payments, and so on. These **functional information systems** evolved independently of one another. Because the work was performed in functional silos, organizations gave little thought to sharing the data among functions or departments. As a

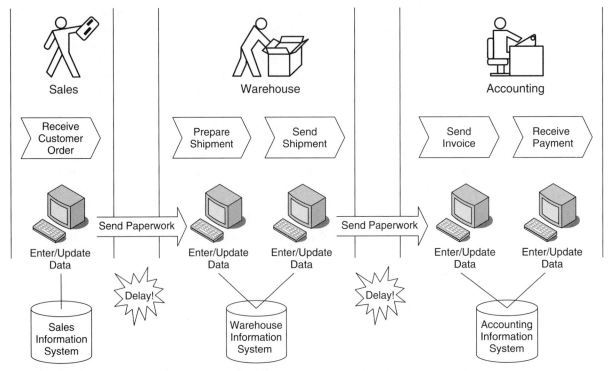

Figure 1.6 A process supported by functional information systems

result, although organizations have implemented systems to support the work of individual functional areas, exchanging information among them is often difficult. To make matters worse, information is often exchanged manually, as Figure 1.6 illustrates. The use of functional information systems has reduced delays associated with maintaining data within the functions. However, the delays associated with communicating with other departments persist because much of this communication still involves paper documents.

1.3.3 Enterprise Systems

Given the complexity of managing the data across entire processes, it is not feasible to rely on manually connecting functional information systems by printing information from one system and rekeying it into the next system. Therefore, in addition to moving from silos to processes, organizations must also move from functionally focused information systems to integrated **enterprise systems** (ES). Enterprise systems support the entire process rather than parts of the process. Put differently, enterprise systems not only support the execution of individual activities in a process, they also help the organization coordinate work across functions. This coordination further reduces delays, avoids excess inventory, and increases visibility. Figure 1.7 illustrates the role of an ES within an organization.

Consider the fulfillment process. When the sales department receives a customer order, it enters the order into the ES and authorizes delivery. People in the warehouse are automatically notified and have access to the information necessary to prepare and ship the order. (Recall that in a manual system, they would have to wait for

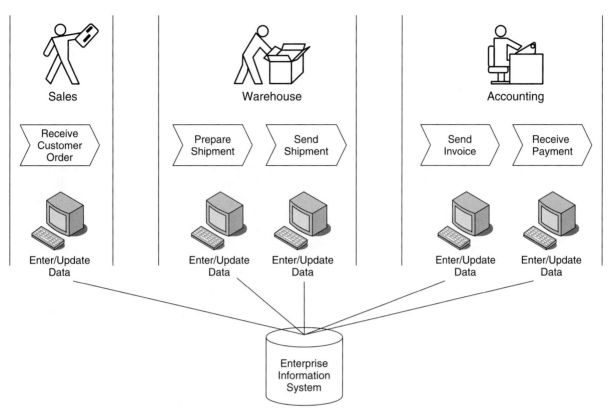

Figure 1.7 A process supported by an enterprise system

the paperwork from sales.) As soon as the order is shipped, accounting receives the information necessary to send the invoice.

An ES can similarly streamline the procurement process. The purchase requisition created in the warehouse is immediately available to the purchasing department, which creates a purchase order and forwards it electronically to a suitable supplier. When the shipment from the supplier is received and the receipt is entered into the system, accounting has immediate access to the information needed to process the invoice when it arrives from the supplier. Thus, there is no need to explicitly communicate this information among functions.

In addition to eliminating the need to communicate explicitly among departments, enterprise systems make processes more efficient by automating some of the routine steps in the process. In the procurement process, for example, when a purchase requisition is created, the ES automatically selects a suitable supplier, creates a purchase order, and sends it to the supplier, based on previously established rules. In the fulfillment process, the ES automatically generates an invoice as soon as a shipment is sent to the customer and electronically send it to the customer.

A final benefit of enterprise systems is that they provide greater visibility across the process. Each person involved in the process has almost instant access to the information about the process. At any time, the system can be queried about the current state of the customer order or purchase requisition, for example, which part of the order fulfillment process is currently being executed, or when the purchase order was sent to the supplier. This increased visibility reduces uncertainty for all concerned parties. For instance, the anxious customer can be assured that the order was shipped this morning, and the anxious warehouse manager can rest easy with the knowledge that the shipment from the supplier will be arriving on time. The reduced delays and increased visibility have a positive impact on lead times, cycle times, inventory, lost sales, and customer service.

1.3.4 Why Is This Information Important to You?

Now that we've discussed processes and enterprise systems, you might be wondering: What does this information have to do with me? Very often students believe that this material is important only to IT majors. This belief is incorrect. Recall our discussion at the beginning of the chapter of the skills possessed by knowledge workers. One of these skills is the ability to think strategically and understand the big picture. At a very fundamental level, this skill requires you to understand the following aspects of an organization:

- How processes are executed within the organization
- How your work supports the execution of the process
- How your failure to perform your work successfully will cause the process to fail
- What you must do well to ensure the process succeeds

Another skill is communication and collaboration, which enables you to work well in project teams. How will you be effective in a cross-functional project team if you do not understand the role others play in the process and how what you do affects them? A final skill is information literacy and the ability to utilize an information system to identify, obtain, and use the necessary information to do your job well. Do you still doubt that information systems are for everyone in the organization and not just the "techies"?

In the next three sections, we will develop a framework to understand processes, the role of enterprise systems, and the financial impact of processes. We will then incorporate this framework throughout the book as we discuss specific processes in greater detail.

► 1.4 FLOWS IN BUSINESS PROCESSES

A process "flows" through different functions in an organization as the various steps needed to complete the process are executed. This flow, which was represented in Figure 1.1, represents the **physical flow** of a process, that is, the physical activities associated with the process. There are additional "flows" associated with a process, which we depict in Figure 1.8. We previously explained that there are data associated with each step of the process, such as dates, quantities, locations, and amounts. These data accompany, or "flow," through the physical steps in a process, and along the way, they are often modified and updated. For example, when a shipment is made against a customer order, the quantity shipped is now associated with the process. Thus, a **data flow** is associated with a process. Going further, the data are often found in documents such as purchase orders and invoices that are created or modified in different steps of a process. These documents can be either physical or electronic. Like data, these documents "flow" along with the process steps. For instance, a customer order accompanies the process steps, and as various steps are completed,

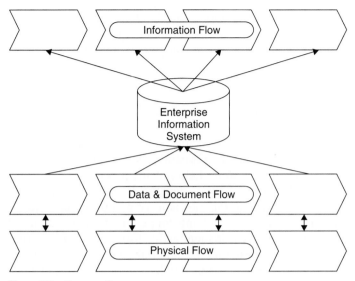

Figure 1.8   Process flows

the order is updated to reflect the completion of steps. This is the **document flow** associated with a process.

Processes are executed multiple times. For example, a company will process numerous customer orders in a day. Each execution of the process is an instance or occurrence of the process. The three flows discussed above are associated with each instance of a process. That is, each time the physical steps in a process are executed, data and documents are created or modified.

One additional flow, **information flow**, is associated with each instance of the process as well as at an aggregate level, that is, across multiple instances or executions of a process. Data generated in each step and across an entire process are accumulated over time. For example, data about numerous customer orders are collected and stored in the ES. These data are then organized in a manner that is meaningful and useful for some purpose, such as creating a report summarizing sales for the previous month. Once the data have been organized into a sales report, managers and employees can analyze problem areas and work together to improve them.

▶ 1.5 THE ROLES OF ENTERPRISE SYSTEMS IN ORGANIZATIONS

As we have seen, enterprise systems are a critical component of the process view of organizations. They facilitate communication and coordination among different functions, and they allow easy exchange of, and access to, data across the process. More specifically, ES play a vital role in the following three areas:

1. Execute the process
2. Capture and store process data
3. Monitor process performance

In this section we discuss each of these roles. In some cases the role is fully automated; that is, it is performed entirely by the system. In other cases the system must rely on the managers' judgment, expertise, and intuition.

1.5.1 Execute the Process

Enterprise systems help organizations execute processes efficiently and effectively. ES are embedded into the processes, and they play a critical role in executing the processes. In other words, the system and the process are intertwined. If the system stops working, the process cannot be executed.

Enterprise systems help execute processes by informing people when it is time to complete a task, by providing the data necessary to complete the task, and in some cases by providing the means to complete the task. In the fulfillment process, for example, the system will inform people in the warehouse that orders are ready for shipment and provide them with a listing of what materials must be included in the order and where to find the materials in the warehouse. In the procurement process, the system generates the purchase requisitions and then informs the purchasing department that they need to act on these requisitions. The accountant will be able to view all shipments received to match an invoice that has been received from a supplier and verify that the invoice is accurate. Without the system, these steps, and therefore the process, cannot be completed. For example, if the system is not available, how will the warehouse know which orders are ready to pack and ship? As you might have concluded by now, because organizations rely so heavily on ES, they must make certain that these systems are functioning all the time so that the work is not interrupted. They also should have extremely good backup systems in case of failure. Business Processes in Practice 1-6 illustrates the dependence of processes on systems in the case of Amazon.com.

1.5.2 Capture and Store Process Data

As we previously discussed, processes create data such as dates, times, product numbers, quantities, prices, and addresses, as well as who did what, when, and where. Enterprise systems capture and store these data, commonly referred to as *process data* or *transaction data*. Some of these data are generated and automatically captured by the system. These are data related to who, when, and where an activity is completed. Other data are generated outside the system and must be entered into

---

▶ *BUSINESS PROCESSES IN PRACTICE 1-6*

AMAZON.COM

Earlier in the chapter we explained that, rather than manufacture its own products, Amazon.com purchases and stores finished goods and then resells them to its customers. Significantly, the company receives most of their orders via their Web site, their online storefront. This Web site is connected to an enterprise system that supports the fulfillment process. When an order is received, the system communicates this information to the warehouse, where the order is packed and shipped.

If the online store stops working, then Amazon.com can't take any orders, and their entire warehouse will come to a stop.

Source: Compiled from: Amazon company reports; "Amazon.com: Evolution of the e-Tailer," March 30, 2001, *Harvard Business School* Case #SM83; and "Amazon.com: The Wild World of e-Commerce," *Business Week*, December 14, 1998.

it. This data entry can occur in various ways, ranging from manual data entry to automated methods involving data in forms such as bar codes that can be read by machines. In the fulfillment process, for example, when a customer order is received (by mail or over the phone), the person taking the order must enter data such as the name of the customer, what they ordered, and how much they ordered. Data such as the name of the person entering the data (who), at which location they are completing this task (where), and the date and time (when) are automatically included by the system when it creates the order in the system. The data are updated as the process steps are executed. When the order is shipped, the warehouse will provide data about what products were shipped and how many, whereas the system will automatically include data related to who, when, and where.

An important advantage of using an ES compared to a manual system or multiple functional systems is that the data need to be entered into the system only once. Moreover, once they are entered, they are easily accessible to other people in the process, and there is no need to reenter them in subsequent steps. The data captured by an ES, along with data already in the system, provide immediate feedback. For example, they can be used to create a receipt or to make recommendations for additional or alternate products. The data are also stored for later use and analysis. Business Processes in Practice 1-7 illustrates the immediate feedback capabilities of an ES.

1.5.3 Monitor Process Performance

A final contribution of enterprise systems is to help to monitor the state of the processes, that is, to indicate how well the process is executing. An ES performs this role by evaluating information about the process. This information can be created either at the *instance level* (i.e., a specific task or activity) or the *process* or *aggregate level* (i.e., the process as a whole). At the instance level, for example, a company might be interested in the state of a particular customer order. Where is the order within the fulfillment process? When was it shipped? Was the complete order shipped? If it has not been shipped, then when can we expect it to be shipped? Or, for the procurement process, when was the purchase order sent to the supplier? What will be the cost of acquiring the material?

At the aggregate level, the ES can evaluate how well the procurement process is being executed by calculating the lead time, or the time between sending the purchase order to a vendor and receiving the goods, for each order and each vendor over time. Figure 1.9 is an example of aggregate-level information regarding the fulfillment process. This figure provides a summary of customer orders for the

---

▶ **BUSINESS PROCESSES IN PRACTICE 1-7**

AMAZON.COM

When a customer purchases something on Amazon.com, the system provides a confirmation number that can be used to track the progress of the order. In addition, the data in the current order are combined with historical sales data to recommend additional products that may be of interest to the customer—resulting in higher sales.

Source: Compiled from: Amazon company reports; "Amazon.com: Evolution of the e-Tailer," March 30, 2001, *Harvard Business School* Case #SM83; and "Amazon.com: The Wild World of e-Commerce," *Business Week*, December 14, 1998.

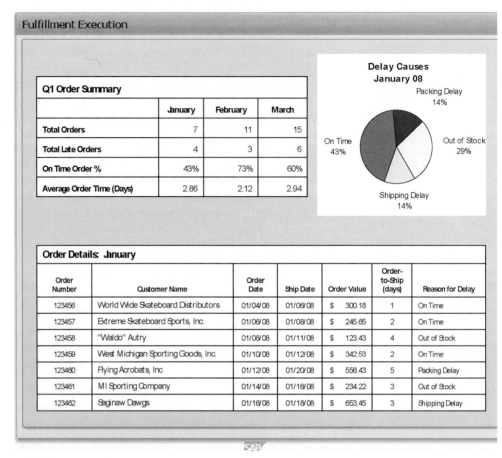

Figure 1.9 Example of process-level information
Source: Copyright SAP AG 2008

months of January, February, and March (top left) as well as detailed information about specific orders (bottom). It also graphically depicts reasons for delays in processing the orders.

Not only can the ES help monitor a process, it can also detect problems with the process. It performs this role by comparing the information with a *standard*—that is, what the company expects or desires—to determine if the process is performing within expectations. Management establishes standards based on organizational goals. If the information provided by the ES indicates that the process is falling short of the standards, then the company assumes that some type of problem exists. Some problems can be routinely and automatically detected by the system, whereas others require a person to review the information and make judgments. For example, the system can calculate the expected date that a specific order will be shipped and determine whether this date will meet the established standard. Or, it can calculate the average time taken to fill all orders over the last month and compare this information to the standard to determine if the process is working as expected.

Monitoring the process, then, helps detect problems with the process. Very often these "problems" are really symptoms of a more fundamental problem. In such cases the ES can help diagnose the cause of the symptoms by providing

AMAZON.COM

By capturing detailed data on each activity in their organization, Amazon can assess multiple factors that cause problems or reduce performance. In many cases the company must look at a problem from many angles to determine how to address it. By comparing similar processes across multiple locations, managers can identify higher-performing teams to determine the key factors for their success. They can also identify lower-performing teams to find areas for improvement.

Source: Compiled from: Amazon company reports; "Amazon.com: Evolution of the e-Tailer," March 30, 2001, *Harvard Business School* Case #SM83; and "Amazon.com: The Wild World of e-Commerce," *Business Week*, December 14, 1998.

managers with additional, detailed information. For example, if the average time to process a customer order appears to be increasing over the last month, this problem could actually be a symptom of a more basic problem. A manager can then dig deeper, or drill down, into the information to diagnose the underlying problem. To accomplish this, the manager can request a breakdown of the information by type of product, customer, location, employees, day of the week, time of day, and so on. After reviewing this detailed information, the manager might determine that there has been a high employee turnover in the warehouse over the last month and that the delays are occurring because new employees are not sufficiently familiar with the process. The manager might conclude that this problem will work itself out in time, in which case there is nothing more to be done. Alternatively, the manager could conclude that the new employees are not being adequately trained and supervised. In this case, the company must take some actions to correct the problem. Business Processes in Practice 1-8 illustrates the performance monitoring capabilities of an ES.

► 1.6 FINANCIAL IMPACT OF PROCESS STEPS

A final component of the framework is used to understand the financial impact the different steps in a process have on the organizations. For example, when a company receives a shipment of material from a vendor, it assumes an obligation to pay the vendor. At the same time, the value of the material (inventory) in the warehouse increases. When the company pays the vendor, the obligation to pay no longer exists. At the same time, the amount of money the company has in the bank is reduced.

Significantly, not all activities have a financial impact. For example, when a customer's order is recorded in the system, there is no immediate financial impact. Nevertheless, to develop a complete understanding of processes—the first step in developing strategic thinking skills—it is necessary to understand their financial impact.

Financial impact is typically viewed through changes in an organization's income statement and balance sheet.[1] An **income statement**, also known as a *profit and loss (P&L) statement*, is a record of revenue and expenses for a specific period of time. An income statement shows how much money the company made (revenue), how much money the company had to spend to produce and sell its goods (expenses), and

---

[1] An in-depth discussion of financial statements is beyond the scope of this book. We provide very simple definitions and explanations necessary to understand the financial impact of processes.

Revenues
    Revenues from Sales
    Other Revenues

    Total Revenues

Expenses
    Cost of Goods Sold
    Selling Expenses
        Advertising
        Commission
        Shipping
        Salaries
        Etc.
    General and Administrative Expenses
        Salaries
        Legal and Professional
        Utilities
        Insurance
        Supplies
        Etc.

    Total Expenses

Net Income = Revenue − Expenses

Figure 1.10   Simple income statement

how much profit the company earned (net income). Typical expenses include the cost of goods sold (what the products that were sold cost the company), advertising, wages, insurance, and utilities. Net income is the difference between revenue and expenses. Figure 1.10 shows a simple income statement. In this book we will concern ourselves only with the highlighted elements of the income statement—revenue from sales and cost of goods sold.

Whereas an income statement provides a picture of a company's financial condition over a period of time, a **balance sheet** indicates the financial condition of a company at a specific point in time. It shows what the company owns (assets), what it owes to others (liabilities), and how much money shareholders have invested in the company (equity). Figure 1.11 shows a simple balance sheet. Assets include cash, accounts receivable or money owed to the company by customers, value of the inventory of finished goods and raw material, fixed assets such as buildings and machinery, and so on. Liabilities include any monies that the company owes to vendors as well as any loans the company must repay. Retained earnings are that part of the company's income that it has not reinvested or distributed to shareholders. They are also liabilities in the sense that they are owed to shareholders. In this book we will concern ourselves only with the highlighted elements of the balance sheet—cash, accounts receivables, the various inventory accounts, accounts payable, and retained earnings.

Assets
> **Cash**
> **Accounts Receivable**
> **Inventory**
>> Raw Materials
>> Semifinished Goods
>> Finished Goods
> Property, Plant, and Equipment
> --
> Total Assets

Liabilities
> **Accounts Payable**
> Loans
> --
> Total Liabilities

Equity
> Shareholders Equity
> **Retained Earnings**
> --
> Total Equity

Total Liabilities + Equity

Figure 1.11   Simple balance sheet

Assets, liabilities, revenues, and expenses are tracked through specific accounts. The collection of these accounts is called a *chart of accounts*. Key accounts relevant to the processes discussed in this book are highlighted in Figure 1.10 and Figure 1.11 and are listed in Figure 1.12. Processes affect the financial position of an organization by offsetting an increase or decrease in one account with a corresponding increase or decrease in a different account (or accounts). These could be two accounts in the balance sheet or one each in the income statement and the balance sheet. For example, when the organization receives payment from a customer, accounts receivable is reduced by the amount of the payment, and cash assets (or money in the bank) are increased by that same amount. When there is a sale to a customer on credit, the accounts receivable account is increased, and the sales revenue account is also increased. Thus, there is not always an increase in one account and a decrease in another.

Sales Revenue
Cost of Goods Sold

Cash
Accounts Receivable
Inventory—Raw Materials, Finished Goods, Semifinished Goods
Accounts Payable

Figure 1.12   Simple chart of accounts

For a process to have a financial impact, it must involve two basic elements: an external entity[2] (a customer or a vendor) and an exchange of value (buy, sell, pay, or get paid). You will learn a great deal more about the financial impact of processes in your accounting courses. For now, we will keep things very simple so that you can focus on the impact of the process rather than the accounting rules for revenues, expenses, and income.

▶ CHAPTER SUMMARY

In this chapter we have introduced a number of concepts, terms, and ideas that will be helpful as we discuss processes in greater detail in later chapters. The key ideas in this chapter are

1. Work in organizations is completed by business processes that consist of various steps that are executed in different parts of the organization. Key processes in an organization are procurement, fulfillment, and production.

2. Working within functions has severe limitations and negative consequences that cannot be tolerated in the current global competitive climate. These problems are caused by the "silo effect" and poor coordination of activities across processes. Common problems are delays, excess inventory, and a lack of visibility across processes.

3. Several "flows" are associated with a process. Physical, data, and document flows are associated with instances or occurrences of processes. Information flow is associated with both the instances of processes and the aggregate process level.

4. Enterprise systems are essential in viewing organizations from a process perspective. Enterprise systems connect the work that is done across the organization and provide coordination, data access, and visibility across the process. They capture process data and help monitor the performance of processes, which can help the organization detect and diagnose problems.

5. Processes have a financial impact on the organization. Financial impact is measured by the impact on financial statements such as the income statement and balance sheet.

▶ LAYOUT OF THE BOOK

To reinforce the concepts presented in this book, we will use the case of a hypothetical manufacturing company, *Super Skateboard Builders (SSB), Inc.*, throughout this book. In addition, we will use *SAP* software, the world's leading provider of enterprise systems, as an example of how ICT support the various business processes. We will explain the nature of SSB and the SAP environment used in this book in Chapter 2. The next three chapters will discuss the three key processes: procurement, fulfillment, and production; these are the typical core processes in most organizations. The final chapter will provide an integrated view of the end-to-end business processes in action.

▶ KEY TERMS

balance sheet	fulfillment process	income statement	physical flow
business process	functional information	information	procurement process
data	systems	information flow	production process
data flow	functional structure	information revolution	silo effect
document flow	global competitive	information systems	
enterprise systems	environment	knowledge worker	

[2]Strictly speaking, this is not correct. There can be an exchange of value internally. For example, paying employee salaries and wages (a human resources process) has an impact on the financial position of the firm. In this book we will only discuss the financial impact due to an exchange in value with an external entity.

▶ REVIEW QUESTIONS

1. What are the reasons for increased global competition? What are the consequences of global competition to organizations?

2. What is meant by the term "information revolution"? What caused this revolution? What are the implications of the information revolution for you?

3. What are knowledge workers? What skills do they possess? Why are they important to organizations?

4. Explain the difference between the functional view and the process view of organizations. Why is the process view important today?

5. What are some of the key business processes in an organization? Do all companies have the same key processes? Why or why not?

6. What is a common organizational structure? Why did this structure evolve? What are the benefits of such a structure?

7. What are the typical functions or departments in an organization? What type of work is done in each of these functions?

8. What are the drawbacks of a functional organizational structure? What negative consequences do they lead to?

9. What are functional information systems? What is their value to organizations? What are their main drawbacks?

10. What are enterprise systems? How do they differ from functional information systems? What is the value of enterprise systems to organizations?

11. What is a business process? Explain the various "flows" associated with a business process.

12. Describe two key financial documents.

13. What is a chart of accounts? How is this related to the two key financial documents?

14. Explain how processes affect the two key financial documents. Under what circumstances does a process step have an impact on a company's finances?

▶ ASSIGNMENTS

1. Research some jobs (online or by talking to people in companies) that require knowledge workers. Describe these jobs and explain how and why knowledge workers are needed to fill these jobs.

2. In this chapter we introduced three key processes—procurement, fulfillment, and production. There are a number of other processes in an organization, such as those related to product development, and managing people. Identify one additional process that is typical in organizations. You may consider an organization you have worked in or the educational institution you are attending. For the process provide the following:

(a) A brief description of the process

(b) The purpose or desired outcome

(c) Steps in the process and the person and functional area responsible for completing the step

(d) Data, document, and information flows associated with the process

(e) The types of inefficiencies (delays, etc.) associated with the manual execution of this process

(f) The role of enterprise systems in supporting this process

3. We have identified one specific enterprise system—SAP ERP. Identify other enterprise systems that are available to organizations, and highlight the relative advantages and disadvantages of each one.

CHAPTER 2

Enterprise Systems

Learning Objectives

After completing this chapter you will be able to:

▶ Describe the different types of enterprise systems (ES) and their roles in managing business processes.

▶ Identify the different vendors that supply ES and analyze their market positions.

▶ Explain the architecture of a typical ES.

▶ Compare and contrast the different types of master data in an ES.

▶ Portray the hypothetical company Super Skateboard Builders (SSB) in terms of its history and growth, products, customers, suppliers, and the types of information systems it uses.

In Chapter 1, we briefly introduced enterprise systems (ES) in the context of the business processes that are discussed in this book. In this chapter, we will explain enterprise systems in greater detail, and we will illustrate their role in managing and executing business processes. We will also describe different types of ES, explain the architecture of a typical ES, and identify the major ES software vendors in the market today. We will introduce you to the world's largest ES vendor, SAP®, in greater detail to improve your understanding of the business model that ES vendors employ and how ES vendors aid companies in managing their specific business processes. Next, we will discuss the various types of data in an ES and how they relate to business processes.

In addition to discussing ES, we will introduce the hypothetical company, Super Skateboard Builders (SSB), Inc., which we will use throughout the book to illustrate how business processes work and how ES support these processes. Finally, we will explain the simulated SAP environment that will be used for the chapter exercises in this book to help you understand how ES support business processes.

▶ 2.1 ENTERPRISE SYSTEMS

In today's competitive global environment, it is difficult to imagine how large companies could function without the aid of ES. Beginning in the 1960s, ES began to play a critical role in automating and managing repetitive, manual activities in large businesses. These systems have evolved from stand-alone systems running on large, expensive computers to packaged applications to distributed systems using cheaper, smaller systems. This evolution is briefly described next and is depicted in Figure 2.1. The three broad stages of evolution include the mainframe environment,

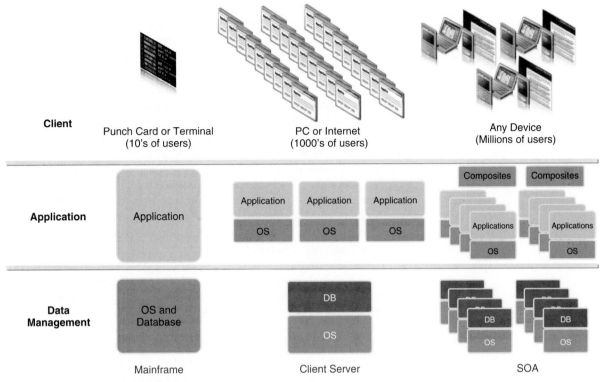

Figure 2.1 The evolution of enterprise systems

client-server systems, and service-oriented architecture (SOA). Each of the stages in this evolution is discussed next.

2.1.1 Stage 1: Stand-Alone Mainframe Systems

Components of an ES include **hardware**, **software**, and a **database**. In the early days of ES, hardware typically consisted of large, expensive mainframe computers. Software includes specialized **operating system** software needed to execute operations from the applications on the hardware and **custom applications** that provide capabilities needed to complete specific tasks, such as filling a customer order. Databases are used to store the data associated with the ES. Early databases were extremely complex and difficult to manage. Only very large companies could afford to acquire and implement an ES. In addition, the way users interacted with the ES was very primitive. They had to use a terminal that was physically connected to the mainframe to input commands to the system using *punch cards* (look it up on Wikipedia). There was no such thing as a computer monitor or a mouse.

For most of the 1960s, 1970s, and 1980s, IBM was the only company that could provide the mainframes, operating systems, and databases for the early ES. For several decades the mainframe architecture was the predominant technology that companies utilized to manage ES. It would take a combination of several innovations in technology and business practices, such as globalization, to break that paradigm and make ES accessible and affordable to a much broader range of businesses.

One of the major drawbacks of the mainframe architecture was its limited **scalability**. Scalability is a concept related to the number of users or the volume of operations that a given hardware/software combination can manage. Scalability is determined by many different aspects of the configuration of a hardware and software combination. In the world of personal computers, you might have experienced situations where you noticed that your computer runs very slowly when a certain application is running or that the performance of a particular video game is especially bad. In these cases, the application (or game) is using a large amount of hardware resources. To increase the scalability of your personal computer to handle the additional workload of the application or game, you could "upgrade" your computer by adding more memory or an improved video processing card. However, in an ES environment this is often very difficult to achieve. Usually, systems are designed to handle a maximum amount of users or operations and are not designed for easy hardware upgrades. Typically, the more scalability (i.e., the number of users or transactions) needed for an application, the higher the upfront costs in hardware, so companies usually purchase the "biggest" hardware they can afford for the job they need to accomplish. In the mainframe architecture, scalability was very low, meaning that only a handful of employees could use the system at any one time. Moreover, the custom application, operating system, and database were entirely contained on a single piece of hardware. This arrangement made increasing scalability prohibitively expensive because of the extremely high costs of bigger mainframe hardware. As a result, companies had to limit both the capabilities and the number of users for each system.

Another limitation of the early ES was that they were *custom designed*, meaning they were designed to address the specific needs of individual firms. Thus, they could not easily be used by other companies. Building a custom system is more expensive than utilizing an existing system, and most small and medium-sized firms could not afford this expense. This is another reason why only the largest companies utilized ES.

In the 1970s, software firms began to develop **packaged applications**. In contrast to proprietary applications that are designed specifically for one firm, packaged applications are generic software that can be used by many companies. By building one version of an ES, the software vendor can spread the cost of software development across many of its customers and thereby reduce the purchase price of the ES for each company. Companies could purchase packaged applications at a fraction of the cost of developing them themselves and then modify them to suit their particular needs. This approach, pioneered by **SAP** in 1972, generated significant cost savings for companies. As a result, the use of ES became much more widespread, at least among large companies.

Although the shift to packaged applications significantly reduced the costs of the total solution, the IBM mainframe hardware, operating system, and database needed to run the packaged application remained very expensive. Thus, the use of ES was still generally confined to larger firms. However, certain technological advances during the 1980s and 1990s led to an increased use of ES. To begin with, hardware and software continued to evolve to become more efficient and capable and less expensive. For example, more advanced operating systems such as UNIX made it easier to manage complex hardware. Similarly, relational databases such as Informix made storing and accessing data much simpler. Another important development was the advent of networking technologies. Companies that are connected to *networks* can access ES remotely rather than having to physically install a system. Ultimately, however, it was the emergence of the **three-tier client-server** architecture that led to the explosive growth in the use of ES.

2.1.2 Stage 2: Client-Server Architecture

Think of a desktop application that you routinely use, such as word processing, spreadsheet, or presentation applications. These applications consist of three components: (1) how you interact with the application (using menus, typing selecting), (2) what the application allows you to do (create formulae or charts, compose an essay), and (3) where the application stores your work (on your hard drive or flash drive). These three components or layers are called the **presentation layer**, **application layer**, and **data layer**, respectively. In the desktop applications mentioned earlier all three layers are contained in one system. In contrast, the three-tier client-server architecture separates these layers into three separate components. This three-tier architecture is illustrated in Figure 2.2. Some systems use a two-tier architecture in which the presentation layer is separated from the application and data layers.

Much of the work you do on the Internet uses either a two-tier or three-tier architecture. Your browser is the presentation layer. You connect to many systems (Web sites) that provide a variety of capabilities (e-mail, information sharing). The Web sites to which you connect combine the application and data layers. Actually,

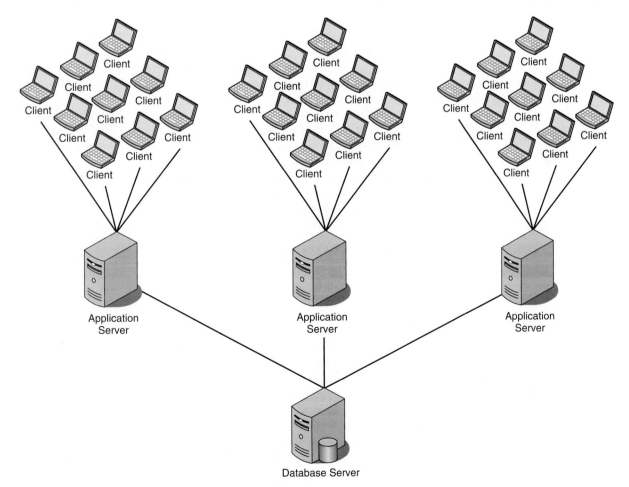

Figure 2.2 The three layers of the client-server architecture

some of these applications use a three-tier architecture by separating the application and data layers, but this is not evident when you use these systems. Another example of a three-tier architecture is instant messaging (IM). When you use IM, you first have to download and install a small piece of software on your computer. This software is the presentation layer, or the user interface to the messaging system that you connect to. It is also the "client" component of the client-server system. The messaging system provides the application layer or the functionality (i.e., the ability to exchange messages with others) as well as the data layer (stores your login information, your contacts, and so on). The messaging system that you connect to is the "server" part of the client-server system.

These examples of three-tier architecture illustrate two key points. First, you have to download and install the presentation layer—that is, the client software—on your computer. This requirement clearly illustrates the separation of the system into parts. If you don't install the client software, you can't use the system. Contrast this to installing a desktop application, where the entire system is installed in one step, because all three layers are combined. Second, you can access the messaging system from any computer that is connected to the Internet. You can do this because the data (your login information and contacts) are stored on the server. This is another indication that the presentation layer is separated from the data and application layers.

Separating the three components in the client-server architecture has enabled ES to achieve much greater scalability and flexibility because the different layers can run simultaneously on different computers rather than exclusively on a single mainframe. Consequently, the ES can be run on considerably cheaper computers. Many companies, such as Sun Microsystems, provide a variety of smaller server computers that are so inexpensive that companies can usually buy several servers for the price of a single mainframe.

By distributing the workload of the application across multiple, smaller application servers, companies can achieve nearly infinite scalability by simply adding more servers. However, to maintain data integrity, each application server has to store its records in a single database that resides on a separate server used solely for the database. Each application server can handle several simultaneous users. Thus, if more users need to utilize an ES, a company simply adds additional application servers to handle the increased workload.

The shift to the three-tier client server dramatically reduced the costs of acquiring, implementing, and using an ES while significantly increasing the scalability of the systems. These two forces transformed ES from a capability that only a few large companies could afford into a technology that tens of thousands of companies can now utilize.

2.1.3 Stage 3: Service-Oriented Architecture

In the early 2000s, companies began to Web-enable their three-tier applications so that users could access the systems through a Web browser. During these years companies also benefited from new technologies that could help link, or *integrate*, many different client-server systems together in new and very valuable ways. These new technologies are collectively labeled **service-oriented architecture**, or **SOA**. By using **Web services**, companies could now integrate several client-server applications and create an enterprise **mashup**, or **composite applications**. Composite applications and mashups rely on Web services to send and receive data between and among ES. In addition, they execute newer and more specific processes than are found in the standard ES.

For example, if your company wants to see the map locations of every customer in San Francisco, you could create a composite application or mashup between the ES that contains your customer data and Google Maps. This new application would take user input for the city and state where you want to locate customers, retrieve the appropriate customer data (customer name, address, city, state, zip code) from the ES via a Web service, and then superimpose the customer addresses onto a Google Map for the users to view. The users have no idea which system the customer data are coming from or how these data are being sent to Google Maps. They simply input the city from which they want customer information, and a map pops up with all the customers' locations highlighted.

Take another example of a Web service involving a purchase of something via a company's Web site, which provides estimated shipping charges from various shipping companies and allows the customer to choose a shipping provider. To do this, the company's enterprise system electronically sends shipment information, such as weight, number of boxes, and the destination zip code, to each of the shipping companies' systems. Once the shipping companies receive the data, their systems instantly provide a quotation, via a Web service, and transmit it back. This information is displayed to the customer, who then chooses a provider. Next the company transmits the final shipping information to the selected shipping provider. The shipping provider then sends a confirmation with the delivery information and tracking number for the shipment, which is provided to the customer. To ensure that the customer does not get frustrated and terminate the order, all of these operations must happen in a few seconds. The systems involved could physically be located on servers sitting on several different continents. Web services provide a standardized and reliable way for multiple systems to communicate in a very fast and scalable way to bring added value and efficiency to a business process.

Companies such as SAP have invested billions of dollars to service-enable their core ES so that these systems can be exposed and connected to an infinite number of composite applications and third-party ES. By using SOA to integrate and expose the business processes and data inside an ES, companies can now create new composite applications quickly and inexpensively. In essence, SOA enables companies to build composite applications on top of their existing three-tier client-server applications without changing the existing applications. This gives companies an entirely new level of flexibility for an extremely low cost.

2.1.4 Types of Enterprise Systems

The paradigm shift in computing architecture occurred simultaneously with the business trends of globalization and business process reengineering (BPR). As companies began to expand their operations globally in the 1980s and began to view organizations from a process view rather than a functional view, BPR emerged in the 1990s as a way to reorient operations around business processes to better manage and control the globally distributed organization.

Enterprise resource planning (ERP) systems

The ES that is most closely associated with the BPR and globalization in the 1990s is **enterprise resource planning (ERP)**. SAP was the first company to create a fully integrated and global ERP system. ERP systems are the world's largest and most complex ES. They focus primarily on the internal operations of an organization, and they integrate functional and cross-functional business processes.

Typical ERP systems include Operations (Production), Human Resources, Finance and Accounting, Sales and Distribution, and Procurement. Thus, ERP systems support processes within a company, or *intracompany processes*. Figure 2.3 shows the solution map for the ERP system developed by SAP. The solution map identifies the functionality and processes supported by the system. This illustration should give you some appreciation for the scope and size of a typical ERP system.

As more companies acquired ERP systems, the next step in the evolution of ES was to connect these systems so they could support *intercompany processes*; that is, processes that take place between and among companies. Examples of connected ES are **supply chain management (SCM)** and **supplier relationship management (SRM)** systems, which connect a company's ERP system to those of its suppliers. SCM connects a company to other companies that supply the materials it needs to make its products. Typical SCM systems help companies plan for their production demand requirements and optimize complex transportation and logistics for materials. SRM systems typically manage the overall relationships with the materials suppliers. SRM systems contain functionality to manage the quotation and contracts processes.

On the other side of the manufacturing and sales process, **customer relationship management (CRM)** systems connect a company's ERP system to those of its customers. CRM systems provide companies with capabilities to manage marketing, sales, and service for its customers. **Product life cycle management (PLM)** systems help companies administer the processes of research, design, and product management. In effect, PLM systems help companies take new product ideas from the virtual drawing board all the way to the manufacturing facility. Figure 2.4 depicts the relationship among the different applications.

The collection of these systems is called an **application suite**. Suite vendors, such as SAP and Oracle, provide fairly comprehensive collections of applications that offer an enormous amount of functionality and cover most of the standard business processes in a company.

End-User Service Delivery					
Analytics	Financial Analytics		Operations Analytics		Workforce Analytics
Financials	Financial Supply Chain Management	Treasury	Financial Accounting	Management Accounting	Corporate Governance
Human Capital Management	Talent Management		Workforce Process Management		Workforce Deployment
Procurement and Logistics Execution	Procurement		Inventory and Warehouse Management	Inbound and Outbound Logistics	Transportation Management
Product Development and Manufacturing	Production Planning		Manufacturing Execution	Product Development	Life-Cycle Data Management
Sales and Service	Sales Order Management		Aftermarket Sales and Service		Professional-Service Delivery
Corporate Services	Real Estate Management	Enterprise Asset Management	Project and Portfolio Management	Travel Management	Environment, Health, and Safety Compliance Mgmt. · Quality Management · Global Trade Services

Figure 2.3 The SAP® ERP solution map
Source: Copyright SAP AG 2008

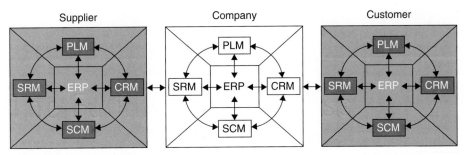

Figure 2.4 The ES application suite

Figure 2.4 identifies the various capabilities that are part of the SAP® Business Suite. To give you a glimpse of the vast scope of the capabilities contained in a suite, Figures 2.5–2.8 are solution maps for SAP® Supply Chain Management (SAP SCM), SAP® Supplier Relationship Management (SAP SRM), SAP® Product Life-cycle Management (SAP PLM), and SAP® Customer Relationship Management (SAP CRM) systems, respectively. It is important to note that one of the key values of having a complete suite of software is that the data and processes are integrated among the systems in the suite. That is, although these are separate systems, they are designed so that they work together in an integrated manner. This setup reduces a great deal of integration cost and effort.

Demand & Supply Planning	Demand Planning & Forecasting	Safety Stock Planning	Supply Network Planning	Distribution Planning	Service Parts Planning
Procurement	Strategic Sourcing		Purchase Order Processing		Invoicing
Manufacturing	Production Planning & Detailed Scheduling		Manufacturing Visibility & Execution & Collaboration	MRP based Detailed Scheduling	
Warehousing	Inbound Processing & Receipt Confirmation	Outbound Processing	Cross Docking	Warehousing & Storage	Physical Inventory
Order Fulfillment	Sales Order Processing		Billing	Service Parts Order Fulfillment	
Transportation	Freight Management	Planning & Dispatching	Rating & Billing & Settlement	Driver & Asset Management	Network Collaboration
Real World Awareness	Supply Chain Event Management			Auto ID / RFID and Sensor Integration	
Supply Chain Visibility	Strategic Supply Chain Design	Supply Chain Analytics	Supply Chain Risk Management	Sales & Operations Planning	
Supply Network Collaboration	Supplier Collaboration		Customer Collaboration	Outsourced Manufacturing	
Supply Chain Management with Duet	Demand Planning in MS Excel				

SAP NetWeaver

Figure 2.5 The SAP SCM solution map
Source: Copyright SAP AG 2008

Purchasing Governance	Global Spend Analysis		Category Management		Compliance Management		
Sourcing	Central Sourcing Hub		RFx / Auctioning		Bid Evaluation & Awarding		
Contract Management	Legal Contract Repository	Contract Authoring	Contract Negotiation	Contract Execution		Contract Monitoring	
Collaborative Procurement	Self-Service Procurement	Services Procurement		Direct / Plan-Driven Procurement		Catalog Content Management	
Supplier Collaboration	Web-based Supplier Interaction		Direct Document Exchange		Supplier Network		
Supply Base Management	Supplier Identification & Onboarding		Supplier Development & Performance Management		Supplier Portfolio Management		

(right vertical label: SAP NetWeaver)

Figure 2.6 The SAP SRM solution map
Source: Copyright SAP AG 2008

Because this is an introductory textbook that focuses on basic business processes, we will discuss only intracompany processes and ERP systems. Keep in mind, however, that the emergence of intercompany business capabilities is one of the most important developments in the modern business environment. However, a fundamental understanding of the key business processes and ERP systems is a prerequisite to advanced topics such as supply chain management and customer relationship management because those processes "feed off" the core ERP-enabled business processes.

Best-of-breed applications

In addition to application suites, today's global companies typically have an ES landscape that includes custom and packaged applications from several vendors. The most common of these applications are **best-of-breed** applications and **niche applications**. Best-of-breed applications are typically isolated to one process or part of a process and have evolved from departmental applications. For example, i2 is a popular supply chain planning system, and Ariba is a popular procurement system. A typical company ES landscape will have one or two core ERP or suite ES plus several best-of-breed applications. Companies need all of these applications because of the silo structure discussed in Chapter 1 and the tendency for each functional

Product Management	Product Strategy and Planning	Product Portfolio Management	Innovation Management	Requirements Management	Market Launch Management	
Product Development and Collaboration	Engineering, R&D Collaboration	Supplier Collaboration	Manufacturing Collaboration	Service and Maintenance Collaboration	Product Quality Management	Product Change Management
Product Data Management	Product Master and Structure Management	Specification and Recipe Management	Service and Maintenance Structure Management	Visualization and Publications		Configuration Management
PLM Foundation	Product Compliance	Product Intelligence	Product Costing	Tool and Workgroup Integration	Project and Resource Management	Document Management

(right vertical label: SAP NetWeaver)

Figure 2.7 The SAP PLM solution map
Source: Copyright SAP AG 2008

Figure 2.8   The SAP CRM solution map
Source: Copyright SAP AG 2008

group to implement its own systems to suit its specific needs. For the company to function effectively, however, all these applications must be tightly integrated.

Niche applications

In addition to the large and medium-sized ES vendors, there are thousands of smaller **independent software vendors (ISVs)** who offer highly specialized niche applications for various industries and functions. Many ISVs build composite applications that sit on top of an ES that was developed by a suite or best-of-breed vendor. These ISV composites frequently take advantage of the technical capabilities of SOA to bridge the gap between ES and provide very useful process capabilities to companies. For example, Vendavo is a small ISV that produces a pricing management tool to assist retailers in maximizing profit for retail sales. Vendavo must pull product and pricing information from several ES to do its job of analyzing pricing conditions to suggest the optimum price for a product. Nakisa is another small ISV who produces a visualization tool that dynamically displays the organizational chart of a company with detailed human resources information. Nakisa must take information from the human resources module of an ERP system and present it in a corporate intranet together with data from an organizational charting tool.

Thus far we have classified ERP systems based on their capabilities. However, ERP systems can also be categorized based on the size of the organization that uses them and the way the system's capabilities are delivered.

Size of the enterprise

Company size can be measured in terms of the number of employees or the company's total revenues. Here we focus on the number of employees. For large enterprises (companies with more than 1000 employees), SAP and Oracle tend to be the most popular vendors based on their scalability and industry-specific functionality. For midsized companies (1000–100 employees), SAP and Oracle are joined by Microsoft and Sage. For small companies (fewer than 100 employees), SAP and Intuit are quite popular.

Method of delivery

Traditional, on-premise ES delivery involves installing the software in a typical three-tier or SOA configuration on physical hardware located at the customer site. Companies purchase the ES software and hardware and then physically install the ES at their facility. In the mid-2000s, a new method of delivery became widespread as companies such as Salesforce.com and NetSuite began to deliver ES solutions entirely from the Web. This delivery model—known as software-as-a-service (SaaS)—enables companies to acquire certain ES functionalities without physically installing software on their servers. SAP also has recently launched a new SaaS version of its software for medium-sized companies called SAP® Business ByDesign.

▶ 2.2 TYPES OF DATA IN ES

So far we have provided a very broad overview of the evolution of ES and the current ES landscape. We now turn our focus to a more specific topic—the types of data in an ES. Data are the heart of any enterprise system. Every step in every process in an organization uses data created in a previous step and, in turn, creates data that will be used in subsequent steps.

The data in an ES are classified into three types: **organizational data**, **master data**, and **transaction data**. Organizational data are used to define the organizational structure of the business, and they rarely change over time. Master data define the key entities with whom an organization interacts, such as customers and suppliers. These data change, but only occasionally. Finally, transaction data reflect the day-to-day activities of the organization. As you might expect, these data are constantly changing. The bulk of the data in an ES consist of transaction data.

Consider the following example: A business sells some of its products to an established customer located in its California sales region. Data about the customers (name, address, etc.) and the product sold (product number, description, weight, etc.) are master data. The region where the sales occurred—California—is organizational data. The details about the sale (quantity, date shipped, etc.) are transaction data. We will discuss these types of data in greater detail in the following sections.

2.2.1 Transaction Data

When an organization completes a specific process activity or task, the data that it generates are transaction data. Transaction data typically include general data such as who did what, when, and where, as well as specialized data that relate to the specific task. For example, when a company sends a purchase order to a vendor, the following transaction data are generated: dates, quantities, name of the person requesting the material, name of the person approving the material, prices, where the shipment is to be delivered, and the shipment method. These data are generated each time a purchase order is created. In general, each time any activity takes place in the organization, data that are specific to that activity are created.

2.2.2 Master Data

Master data describe the key entities associated with an organization. Typical entities are customers, vendors, products, and employees. Master data for customers and vendors include name, address, contact person, and a variety of negotiated terms such as billing and payment methods. For products, master data include product number, description, physical characteristics such as weight and color, handling requirements (e.g., fragile), and typical storage location. Employee master data include name, address, position data, payroll data, tax-related data, and benefits data.

Unlike transaction data, master data are not connected to a specific process or process step. However, process steps require master data to be completed. In fact, master data are used repeatedly in executing processes. For example, if master data don't exist for a customer, then the company can't create a sales order for that customer until it generates a new master record.

Just as master data are utilized across many processes, they also typically involve multiple functional areas. (Recall our discussion of the process and functional areas in Chapter 1.) Significantly, each of these functions defines or views the entity (e.g., customer) differently and uses these data differently. For example, with regard to customer master data the sales department maintains data such as address, contact person, and negotiated terms, and the accounting department maintains data about payment history and credit ratings.

Because the master data are shared across multiple functional areas, it is critical that a company maintain a single version of these data that is complete, accurate, and up to date. As a very simple example, consider what happens if sales and accounting each maintain their own version of a customer's data. If the customer's address changes, this change has to be made in both places. What happens if accounting fails to make this change and instead retains the old address? In that case sales will ship the goods to the customer, but the invoice will not be sent to the correct address. The company will then experience delays in receiving payment. Clearly, then, a single definition of data across the organization is essential to maintain consistency and accuracy.

2.2.3 Organizational Data

Figure 2.9 shows an organizational structure for a hypothetical company. This structure defines the way the different activities of the business are organized. In our example, the company has one global manufacturing operation and two sales operations. The manufacturing or production operation has facilities, or plants, in three locations: China, Mexico, and India. Sales operations are located in North America and the European Union. Sales operations are further divided into wholesale and retail divisions for both regions plus online sales activities for North America. This organizational structure is typically broken down into greater detail.

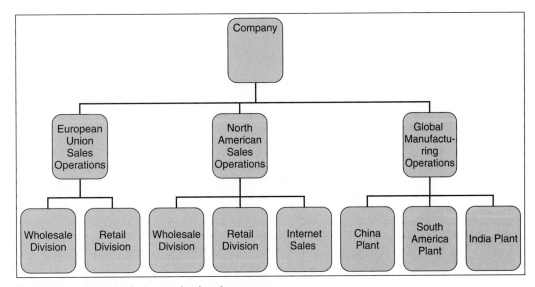

Figure 2.9 A hypothetical organizational structure

For example, each of the production regions includes multiple factories in specific locations. In turn, each factory has various structures such as storage areas, shipping points, and receiving points.

All these data are organizational data and are included in the ES as part of the *configuration* process. Configuration is the process of setting up the ES so it can support the work of the business, that is, the business processes. Many other activities are involved in configuring an ES besides defining the organizational structure. A discussion of these activities is beyond the scope of this book. Our primary objective in this discussion is to explain the concept of organizational data. In the next section we examine master data and transaction data in greater detail as they apply to a specific company.

▶ 2.3 SUPER SKATEBOARD BUILDERS (SSB), INC.

Super Skateboard Builders (SSB), Inc.[1] was founded in 1997 by John "Z-boy" Boeve, the current president of the company, with the help of a small trust John received from his maternal grandmother, a woman who motivated John to go to college and to continue to pursue his skateboarding passion. She marveled at John's skateboarding finesse and encouraged him to find some way to earn a reasonable living by capitalizing on his passion for the sport. John used the money from the trust to buy the necessary shop and office equipment (storage bins, an assembly table, desks, etc.) and lease a small building that would adequately house a skateboard assembly operation. (See Figure 2.10 for a layout of the facilities.) In addition, John invested in some computer equipment and basic office software. He was a strong believer in using the computer to store and track information related to any of life's worthwhile pursuits, especially if they were data-intensive—as he assumed the operation of his new company would be.

Over the next decade SSB grew rapidly. Although this growth was due in part to John's national name recognition—in high school and college he had racked up many awards competing across the country in skateboarding events—the main reason for the company's success was John's leadership, his vision, his management style, and his perseverance.

2.3.1 Product Line

At the present time, SSB has four products. In SAP terminology, these products are trading goods, meaning they are simply purchased in their final form from a supplier and then sold to other retailers or distributors. As you can see in Table 2-1, SSB's four products are entry-level skateboards, helmets, T-shirts, and first aid (repair) kits for skateboards. With current sales exceeding $5 million, SSB is finding it hard to keep up with demand, even though they now employ twice as many workers as when they started. To meet this growing demand, John is considering manufacturing some skateboards in house instead of simply reselling skateboards made by SSB's suppliers.

[1]The SSB case and the various exercises and assignments included in this book are based on the efforts of several faculty members in the Seidman College of Business, Grand State University, that were funded by grants by the Seidman College of Business. We acknowledge efforts of the Seidman faculty and are grateful to the Seidman College for granting us permission to use the data in this book.

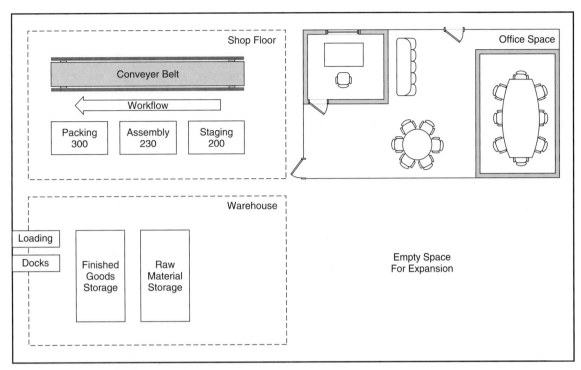

Figure 2.10 SSB plant layout

2.3.2 Customers

SSB sells its products only to retailers who then resell the products directly to consumers. Thus, SSB is a wholesaler. Presently SSB has seven major customers. Master data about these customers are shown in Table 2-2.

2.3.3 Vendors (Suppliers)

As the company's sales increased, it began dealing with a wider variety and number of vendors to supply SSB with the necessary products. Currently SSB deals with seven suppliers on a regular basis. Table 2-3 lists SSB's vendors.

TABLE 2-1 SSB Product List

Product Number	Product Description	Purchase Cost	Selling Price (Wholesale)	MSRP
ENSB3000	Entry-Level Skateboard	$34.00	$45.00	$75.00
HLMT5000	Helmet	$20.00	$27.00	$45.00
SHRT4000	T-Shirt	$7.00	$10.00	$16.00
FAID6000	Skateboard First Aid Kit	$10.00	$16.00	$27.00

TABLE 2-2   SSB Customer List

Customer Number	Name	Address	City	State	Zip
1	World Wide Skateboard Distributors	1229 Main Street	Ann Arbor	MI	48109
2	Extreme Skateboard Sports, Inc.	5000 Rensellear Ave	Detroit	MI	48202
3	"Waldo" Autry	3012 Haslett Road	Lansing	MI	48906
4	West Michigan Sporting Goods, Inc.	6903 28th Street	Grand Rapids	MI	49508
5	Flying Acrobats, Inc.	274 Adams Street	Holland	MI	49423
6	MI Sporting Company	3000 Alpine Ave	Grand Rapids	MI	49544
7	Saginaw Dawgs	4005 State Street SE	Saginaw	MI	48710

2.3.4 Employees

As we explained, although SSB is enjoying unexpected success, it is also having a difficult time handling this rapid growth. When the company was small, all the work was done by five people—John, Maria, and three people in the plant. John and Maria handled all the purchasing and accounting tasks, while Catherine, the plant manager, also supervised the warehouse. Much of the work was done informally. For example, when a customer order came in, it was handled—but no one could explain exactly how. When the company needed material from its suppliers, Catherine just figured out what they needed and called a supplier to order it.

As SSB expanded, John hired additional people to handle sales and purchasing and to manage the warehouse activities. The current organizational chart is shown in Figure 2.11. As the number of employees increased, coordinating their work became more important and also more challenging. In the early years John knew what was going on in the entire company. As the company expanded, however, it became more and more difficult to keep up with the activities of all the employees as well as the ever-increasing volume of customer orders, purchases, and so on.

TABLE 2-3   SSB vendors

Vendor Number	Vendor Name	City	State	Zip
100000	Nutcase Supplies	Grand Rapids	MI	49525
100001	Skatelubbers, Inc.	Grand Rapids	MI	49525
100002	Grand Skateboard Supplies	Grand Rapids	MI	49525
100003	Black Widow Skateboards, Inc.	Holland	MI	49424
100004	Spotted Owl Lumber	Cascade	MI	49546
100005	Van Go Paint Supplies	Kentwood	MI	49508
100006	The Dutch Monster	Grand Rapids	MI	49504
100007	Whitewater Development Company	Jonesboro	AR	72401

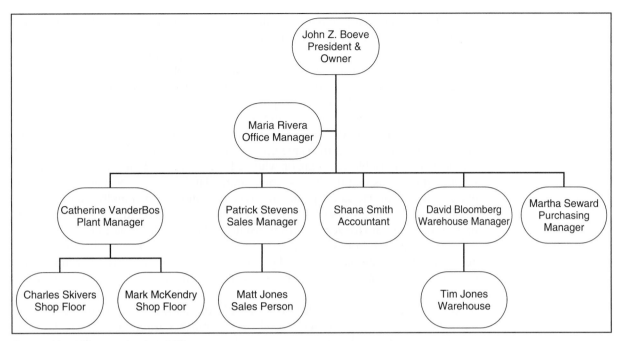

Figure 2.11   SSB organizational chart

2.3.5 Information Systems

For years the company had utilized three stand-alone (not networked) computers, each of which ran the same popular office suite. Using spreadsheets and some databases that John had cobbled together, they had managed to enter all pertinent information and keep track, somewhat accurately, of orders, suppliers, and inventory. Under this arrangement the employees often had to run from computer to computer to swap files with one another on floppy disks to be certain that everyone had the latest version of this or that database or spreadsheet.

John was aware that this system was a disaster waiting to happen. For example, SSB once had used the wrong version of the inventory file to make decisions about ordering materials. As a result they ordered far too many helmets. At first they reassured themselves that this was not really a problem because they eventually would sell the inventory. However, it soon became apparent that the extra helmets took up valuable storage space that could have been used for materials that were needed right away. For a short time some of the extra helmets were actually stored in John's office and in the break room. In addition, shortly after these excess helmets arrived and were paid for, John had to exercise a line of credit to pay for other materials that were needed immediately. Paying for the excess inventory had depleted the company's cash reserves. Exercising the line of credit solved the cash problem, but it also forced the company to incur unnecessary interest charges.

Maria was also having difficulty with the accounting. John's spreadsheets and databases were of little help when it came to keeping the books. Maria was always scrambling to translate the data in these files into information she could then reenter into the accounting software she was using. Data in her system never seemed to be in sync with the files John had set up. One step John took to alleviate this problem was to hire a full-time accountant—Shana—to manage the books. This also freed up Maria's time to better manage the office.

Faced with these and other problems, John sought to apply some of what he had learned in his information system courses in college. He decided to upgrade the computer systems to eliminate having multiple versions of data on different machines and to enable all his employees to share information more efficiently and effectively. All the computers in the company were networked, and a leading enterprise system—SAP—was implemented. The expectation was that everyone now would have access to the same information—no more running around trading spreadsheets or double-checking on who had the version with the latest information. An added plus was that the books would immediately reflect any changes that took place with inventory, sales, payments, receipts, and so on. Finally, the company would be able to do away with Maria's old independent accounting system, meaning that Maria would no longer have to translate and reenter information.

John had high hopes for the new system. Of course, the hard part was just beginning. Everyone had to learn how to use the system, not just in terms of the mechanics but, more important, in terms of how the system would support their work. More specifically, every employee had to understand the various business processes that SSB executed, his or her part in these processes, and the role of the new ES in enabling these processes. There was much learning to be done. College had not quite prepared John to view his company from a process perspective.

We will use SSB as a running example throughout this book to illustrate how key processes work in an organization. We will explain how the different people in SSB are involved in the processes, what their role is, how they interact with others in the organization and how they are dependent on each other to ensure the smooth execution of processes. We will also consider many examples of the negative consequences that occur when SSB adopts a silo view rather than a process view. Ultimately, it is our goal to use the SSB example to make clear to you importance of the skills identified in Chapter 1—strategic thinking, communication, collaboration, and information literacy.

We will be using the ES developed by SAP to illustrate the role of such systems in supporting processes. We will not be using an actual ES; rather, we will use a simulated version of the system. A simulation will allow you to focus on the processes and how they are executed in an ES without having to learn how to use specific software.

We next provide a brief history of SAP, followed by an explanation of how the simulated version of SAP's ES will be used in the book.

▶ 2.4 SAP OVERVIEW

Over the course of more than three decades, SAP has evolved from a small, regional enterprise into a world-class international company. In 2008, SAP was the global market leader in ES solutions. Given SAP's enormous global customer base, it is highly likely that at some point during your career you will work in a company that runs SAP software. The evolution of SAP as a company is briefly described next and is depicted in Figure 2.12. Because SAP is a German corporation, all its financial statements are denominated in euros, the currency used by the majority of the European Union member nations.

In 1972, five former IBM employees launched a company called **S**ystems **A**pplications and **P**roducts in Data Processing in Mannheim, Germany. SAP is

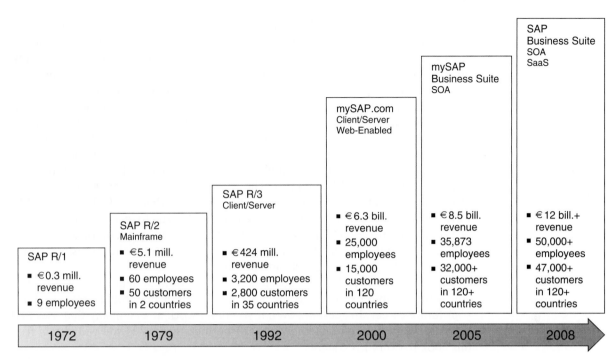

Figure 2.12 The evolution of SAP
Source: SAP AG 2008

the acronym for the original name of the company, and each letter is pronounced individually, just like IBM or ABC. Their vision was to develop standard application software for real-time business processing. After a year of development, they introduced their first financial accounting software, which formed the basis for what later came to be known as the "R/1 system." "R" stood for real-time data processing. R/1 was an ES based on the IBM mainframe architecture. Users utilized punch cards to execute transactions in the system. By the end of the 1970s, SAP had expanded the capabilities of R/1 significantly. In addition, the company introduced a new, more powerful product called SAP R/2, which could take advantage of the first text-only video terminals for user inputs.

In the early 1980s, SAP moved into a new headquarters located in the tiny town of Walldorf, Germany, near Heidelberg, where it still has its global headquarters today. By this time, 50 of the 100 largest German industrial firms were already SAP customers. In order to expand throughout the rest of Europe, SAP designed SAP R/2 to handle different languages and currencies—a revolutionary capability in those early days of enterprise software. Then, in 1992, SAP developed a new ERP solution known as SAP R/3 that was based on the three-tier client-server architecture. The client-server concept, which provided uniform appearance of graphical user interfaces, consistent use of relational databases, and the ability to run on computers from different vendors, met with overwhelming approval from customers. With SAP R/3, SAP ushered in a new generation of enterprise software. To this day, the client-server architecture is the standard in business software.

In late 1999, SAP introduced its new suite of products, which included SAP CRM, SAP SRM, SAP SCM, and SAP PLM applications. These extended capabilities provided companies with collaborative tools to work with their partners and customers on extended business processes. Recall that ERP systems focus on optimizing business processes within a company (intracompany). Collaborative applications, such as the SAP Business Suite, focus on optimizing processes that involve interactions between companies (intercompany) and their customers and partners. With the global adoption of the Internet, the SAP Business Suite could now manage nearly every business process for a company's entire worldwide operations.

In the early 2000s, SAP began to Web-enable the SAP Business Suite of applications and rearchitect them to SOA standards. In 2007, SAP delivered the world's first SOA-based ES suite. It also provided several new capabilities for its customers to create composite applications. Today, more than 12 million users work each day with SAP solutions. The company has almost 50,000 customers in 120 countries, and its products are installed on more than 120,000 servers. SAP's software is translated into 33 languages and is customized to meet the specific needs of 25 major industries. SAP is the world's third-largest independent software vendor, behind Microsoft and Oracle. Perhaps more important, it is the largest enterprise software vendor, ahead of Oracle and Microsoft.

Although this textbook is not an actual SAP training manual, it will provide you with valuable exposure to the SAP ERP system that could prove useful in your future career. In addition, even if you don't work at a company that uses SAP software, you can apply the knowledge of business processes you will obtain from this book to every ES system.

► 2.5 SAP SOFTWARE (SIMULATION)

To make the concepts discussed in each chapter of this book more real to you, we have included a simulated SAP ERP environment where you will also have the opportunity to execute all the process steps discussed in each chapter. Hopefully, you will become aware of the significant advantages of process execution in ES compared to the manual, or paper-based world.

The simulated SAP environment is based on the actual SAP ERP system that is used by more than 50,000 of the world's best-managed companies. However, because the goal of this textbook is to help you master business process concepts and not to master the ES software, we have simplified the user interface and transactional capabilities significantly.

You will access the simulations via WileyPLUS, and your professor will direct you to the assignments. NOTE that you must already have registered for WileyPLUS using a registration code that came packaged with this text. (If you bought a used textbook, you may need to purchase a registration code seperately. For more information about buying a registration code, see the Preface of this book, in the section titled "WileyPLUS - Information for Students.")

The simulations are accessible from nearly any computer with Adobe Flash version 9 or later installed in your browser. We have tested the simulations with Firefox, Safari, and Internet Explorer. Other browsers should work, but if you have problems, please use one of the tested browsers (they're all free).

You will see that Chapters 2 through 6 have exercises that your instructor can assign. These exercises consist of two parts plus a quiz. The first part is a guided tour of the process or information related to that chapter of the textbook. This guided tour will show you where to click to find information, where to input data, and how to complete the process. There will be several windows with details and explanations of each step. Pay very close attention to the guided exercise! You will need this information for the second part of the exercises.

In the second part you will complete the exercise on your own, without any help or hints. It will include the same steps and activities as the guided exercise, but some of the information used in the guided practice will be changed a bit. The exercise is designed to help you learn how processes are executed but to prevent you from making mistakes. You must click in the right spot or enter the right information to proceed to the next step. If you pay attention in the guided practice, you should not experience any trouble completing the second part on your own.

In addition, your professor may assign you to complete a short quiz about the simulations you just completed. This quiz will be found in the Assignments area of WileyPLUS. These questions are fairly simple, but you must pay attention during the practice and exercise to get the answers right. We recommend that you complete the entire series of practice, exercise, and quiz in one sitting to maximize your learning opportunity.

Let's get started with the exercises! In this chapter we have introduced SSB. The exercises will ask you to retrieve and review a variety of master data from our simulated system. In particular, you will retrieve master data related to customers, vendors, and products. Remember, you will first complete the guided exercise and then complete a similar exercise on your own. Finally, you will take a short quiz. After you have completed the quiz, the system will grade it and send your score to your professor's grade book. You may view your score in the gradebook tab of WileyPLUS. Please check with your instructor as to his or her requirements with respect to the simulated exercises. Note that you may repeat these exercises as often as is necessary to thoroughly understand the master data in our simulated system.

▶ CHAPTER SUMMARY

In this chapter we have considered several aspects of enterprise systems and their role in managing business processes. We have described the evolution of ES from the early days of expensive mainframe systems through the paradigm shift to cost-effective and scalable three-tier client-server applications to today's SOA-based systems.

Enterprise systems can be understood by looking at the functionality they contain. Suites and best-of-breed and niche applications are utilized in most companies today. Suites have the advantage of containing most of the business processes needed to run a company in a tightly integrated package. Best-of-breed solutions tend to have slightly better functionality, but come with the added cost of integrating with other applications and systems. Niche applications are provided by smaller ISVs who build on top of or in between suites and best-of-breed applications to address very specific business processes in companies.

ERP systems are the heart and soul of most companies' ES landscape. ERP processes are extended and complemented by CRM, SCM, SRM, and PLM functionality to collaborate with suppliers and customers.

We reviewed the history of the world's leading ES provider, SAP. SAP's growth and expansion ran parallel with the evolution and adoption of ES solutions around the world. SAP has grown from a tiny German software provider to become the world's largest ES vendor. Nearly every major company in the world depends heavily on SAP solutions to manage their business.

Process steps executed in an ES depend on master data, which are data about key entities such as customers, materials, and vendors. Transactional data are captured at every step of the process to record all the relevant information about what was done in each step. These data are later used to help improve and manage the process. Organizational data are used to define the organizational structure of the company.

We also discussed Super Skateboard Builders (SSB), Inc., the fictional company that we will use throughout this book to illustrate how companies execute the basic business processes. SSB is a wholesaler of skateboards and skating products. It is considering starting to make skateboards rather than simply buying from a vendor and reselling. SSB uses information systems to manage its relationships with vendors, customers, and employees.

▶ KEY TERMS

application layer	enterprise resource	organizational data	software
application suite	planning (ERP)	packaged applications	supplier relationship
best-of-breed	hardware	presentation layer	management (SRM)
composite applications	independent software	product lifecycle	supply chain
custom applications	vendors (ISVs)	management (PLM)	management (SCM)
customer relationship	mashups	SAP	three-tier client-server
management (CRM)	master data	scalability	transaction data
data layer	niche applications	service-oriented	Web services
database	operating system	architecture (SOA)	

▶ REVIEW QUESTIONS

1. Describe the differences among the three generations of enterprise systems—mainframe architecture, client-server architecture, and service-oriented architecture.

2. Explain the functions of the different systems in an application suite. How are they related?

3. What are the roles of organizational data, master data, and transaction data in an ES?

4. What functional areas are included in SSB's organizational structure? Is this a common organizational structure? Draw the organizational structure of a small or medium-sized company that you are familiar with.

5. Describe the key problems SSB faced with its use of technology to manage its operations before it implemented an enterprise system. How can the ES improve SSB's operations?

▶ ASSIGNMENTS

1. Provide two examples of organizational data, master data, and transaction data within the context of your university or another organization you are familiar with.

2. Service-oriented architecture (SOA) is touted as a technology that will drastically change the way organizations utilize enterprise systems. Research the use of SOA in organizations, and argue whether SOA will be the next major technological development.

3. In this chapter we provided you with examples of vendors that provide suite, best-of-breed, and niche applications. Conduct your own research, and develop a list of vendors and the types of applications they develop.

CHAPTER 3

The Procurement Process

CHAPTER

Learning Objectives

After completing this chapter you will be able to:

▶ Describe the steps in the procurement process.

▶ Explain the role of different functional areas in efficiently and effectively completing the procurement process.

▶ Identify the key steps in the procurement process and the data, document, and information flows associated with the process.

▶ Explain the financial impact of the steps in the procurement process.

▶ Explain the role of enterprise systems in supporting the procurement process.

When John Boeve started SSB, Inc., he used his connections from his competitive skateboarding days to help him get started. Initially, when sales were modest, he was able to simply call a supplier he knew and ask him to send some products. Over time, however, SSB grew more rapidly than John had anticipated. Today the company has expanded to the point where John can no longer manage all the purchasing himself. He needs a more formal way to order the products that he needs and to keep track of which goods SSB received and how much it owes to its suppliers. In other words, John needs to define a procurement process for SSB.

A **procurement process** is a series of steps that a company takes to obtain or acquire necessary materials. It is also referred to as the *requisition-to-pay* process. The term *materials* can have two meanings. For firms that manufacture their own goods, the materials tend to be the raw materials or supplies from which the goods are made. In contrast, for resellers, the materials are trading goods that are already manufactured. SSB is in the process of transitioning from a reseller to a manufacturer.

In this chapter, we will first consider a simple procurement process in terms of the various flows introduced in Chapter 1—physical, data, document, and information. We will identify the steps in the process and the functional areas involved in each step. We will also examine the various documents, data, and information involved in the procurement process. Next, we will consider the financial impact of the various steps in the process. We will conclude the chapter by demonstrating how companies today use enterprise systems to help execute the process, capture the data generated in the process, and monitor the state of the process.

▶ 3.1 KEY CONCEPTS AND ASSUMPTIONS

Purchasing in business is quite different from the way that individuals acquire goods. When individuals need to buy something, they can easily go to a store or Web site, purchase the products they need, and pay by cash, check, or credit card. In contrast, for many financial, operational, and legal reasons, companies cannot simply go down to the store and buy what they need. Rather, they must purchase most of their materials directly from other companies according to business requirements. We refer to these transactions as **business-to-business (B2B) commerce**. As we saw in the case of John's company, B2B commerce requires a standardized process for buying and selling commercial goods and also for transferring funds to pay for those goods in an efficient manner.

The relationship between a supplier and a customer in the business-to-business world is very different from the relationship between a retailer and a consumer. In the latter case, if a consumer goes to a store looking for a certain product and the store is out of stock, the consumer can simply go to another store. He or she has no legal or financial obligation to buy anything at that store, and the store has no legal or financial obligation to sell the consumer the product or advise him or her promptly if the product is not available. If the item is in stock, then the consumer will pay with a credit card, cash, or a check. These are simple financial transactions. Therefore, the retailer does not need to have any established relationship with the consumer before the purchase is made.

Once a company begins to depend on another company for its critical materials, however, the level of risk increases significantly for both parties. From the buyer's perspective, if the supplier cannot provide the materials when the buyer needs them, then, unlike an individual consumer, the buyer cannot simply walk or drive to another supplier. From the supplier's perspective, because the amount of money for each purchase is significant and purchases are repeated weekly or monthly for many years, the supplier must be certain that the company purchasing its products can promptly pay for them. Now, imagine that these two companies are located in different parts of the world, with different currencies, tax systems, and tariffs and duties to deal with. It should be obvious, then, that even a simple B2B transaction can get very complicated and very risky, very quickly. For this reason, it is critical that companies establish a legally binding and financially secure relationship before they start doing business.

Because the relationship between suppliers and customers in the business-to-business world is so complex, it is essential that detailed and standardized processes be put into place to ensure that both companies can minimize their exposure to risk in the relationship. Relationships might be built on trust, but limiting exposure to risk is extremely important for companies to do business efficiently across the globe.

▶ 3.2 A BASIC PROCUREMENT PROCESS

In Chapter 1 we introduced the concept of flows associated with processes—physical, data, document, and information—as well as a framework to understand the financial impact of the overall process on the organization. In this chapter we look more specifically at how these flows apply to the procurement process. In Chapters 4 and 5 we will consider these same flows in the context of the fulfillment and production processes.

We begin our discussion with a basic procurement process to understand the key flows in the process. Figure 3.1 illustrates the different functional areas in the

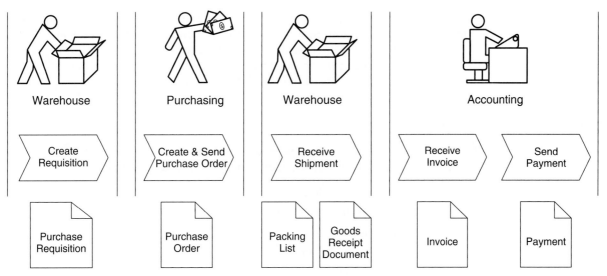

Figure 3.1   A basic procurement process

organization that are involved in the process, the steps that comprise the process, and some of the documents associated with the process.

The procurement process begins when a company discovers that it needs to acquire materials such as office supplies, parts in the warehouse, or anything else it uses. For material stored in the warehouse—such as raw material and trading goods—the need to acquire material is determined by the person responsible for managing inventory, that is, for ensuring that the organization always has an adequate supply of material. In our discussion, we will assume that this responsibility lies in the warehouse.

3.2.1 Physical Flow

The procurement process begins with a request to purchase material created by David Bloomberg, the warehouse manager. (See "*create requisition*" in Figure 3.1). David must ensure that all the products are available in stock in sufficient quantities. When quantities fall below a certain level, David forwards a requisition to Martha in purchasing, where multiple requests can be consolidated. Martha will select a suitable vendor and send a purchase order ("*create & send purchase order*"). The vendor will send a shipment containing the ordered material, which is received by Tim in the warehouse ("*receive shipment*"). The receiving step involves verifying the contents of the shipment. It can also include other steps such as quality inspection and storing the material in the right locations. The vendor then sends a bill, or invoice, for the material shipped. This invoice is received by Shana in accounting ("*receive invoice*"), who will verify its accuracy and send a payment to the vendor ("*send payment*").

It is important to understand how the different people involved in the procurement process know when it is time to do their part. How does Martha know when to send the purchase order to the vendor? When Tim receives a shipment in the warehouse, how does he know which purchase order to match it with? How can he determine whether the materials in the shipment are correct? How does Shana know if the invoice she received is valid and should be paid? Companies use a variety of documents to keep track of the data associated with each of the steps in a process. In addition, in a manual environment, these documents are used to communicate with the other parties involved in the process. In the following section we will discuss some of the more common documents associated with procurement and the key data elements contained in these documents.

3.2.2 Document and Data Flow

Figure 3.1 also identifies the common documents associated with the procurement process. SSB uses the following documents in its procurement process:

1. Purchase requisition
2. Purchase order
3. Packing list
4. Goods receipt document
5. Vendor invoice
6. Vendor payment

In this section we examine each of these documents and the data associated with them.

Purchase Requisition

In a manual environment, David will physically monitor the quantity of products on the shelves in the warehouse. When the quantity is reduced to some predetermined level, he will create the **purchase requisition** (Figure 3.2). A purchase requisition is a document that identifies the material needed, the quantity needed, and the date it is needed. In our example, David creates the requisition displayed in Figure 3.2. It identifies David as the person preparing the requisition, and it specifies that he wants the products in the warehouse by July 27 (area 1 in Figure 3.2). It also specifies the products needed—skateboards, helmets, T-shirts, and first aid kits—along with the desired quantity of each one (area 2). Area 3 will be completed in a subsequent step when the purchase order is created; we will discuss this step later. Finally, each requisition is identified by a unique *requisition number*. Later, when the purchase order is created, a unique *purchase order number* will be added (area 5). The company can use this number to retrieve information about the requisition and to determine its status.

After creating the requisition, David sends it to Martha in the purchasing department for further processing. He will keep a copy for his records and file it in the warehouse office.

Purchase Order

When the purchasing department receives the requisition, it selects a suitable supplier and creates a **purchase order** (Figure 3.3). A purchase order is an agreement to purchase the stated material, for the stated price, under the stated *terms*. Because it commits the organization to the purchase, all purchases typically must be processed by the purchasing department to ensure that they comply with the company's purchasing policy. A purchase order contains much of the data found in the purchase requisition, including the type and quantity of the materials ordered. In addition, it contains pricing and shipping information.

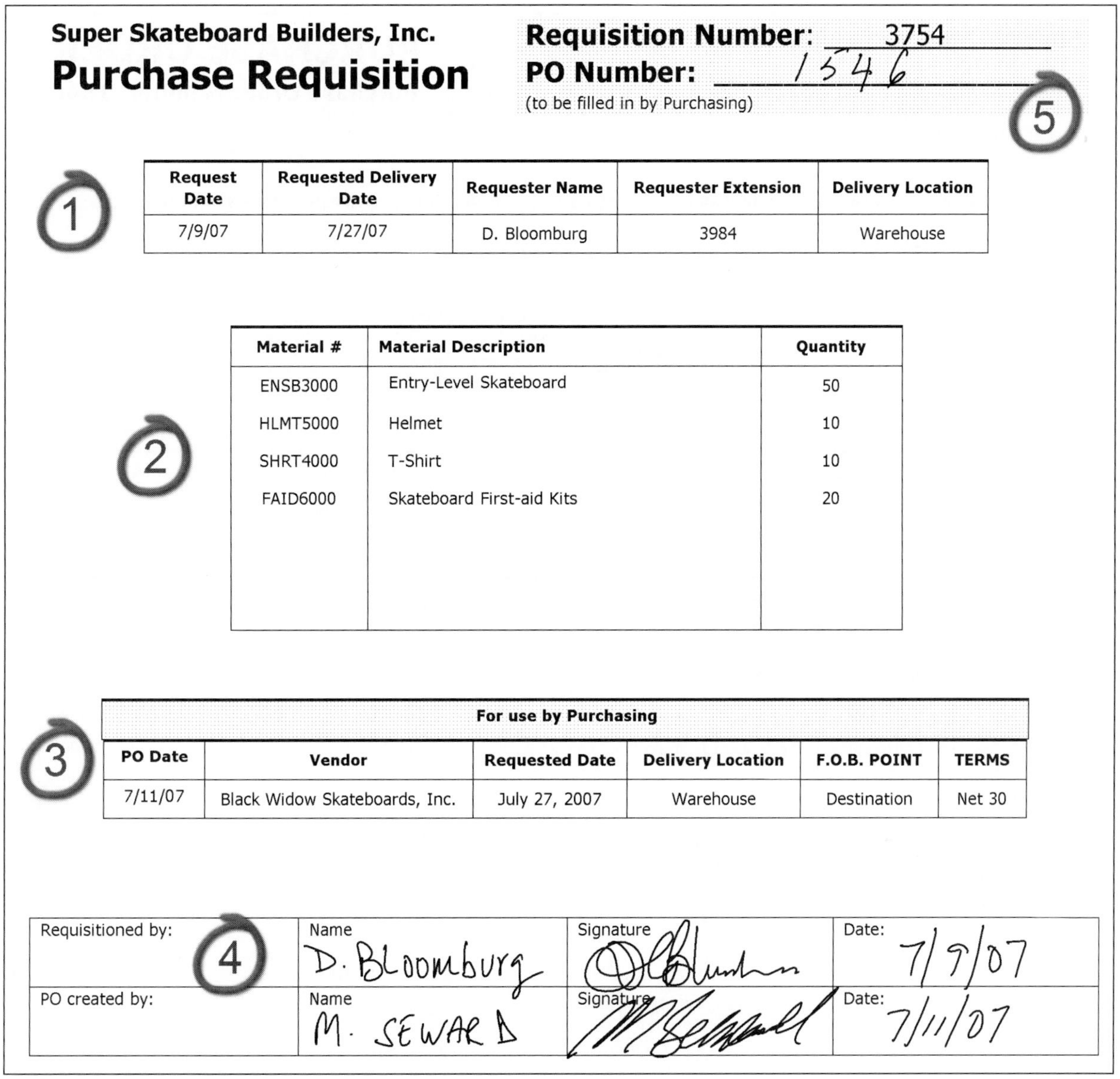

Super Skateboard Builders, Inc.
Purchase Requisition

Requisition Number: _____ 3754 _____
PO Number: _____ 1546 _____
(to be filled in by Purchasing)

⑤

①

Request Date	Requested Delivery Date	Requester Name	Requester Extension	Delivery Location
7/9/07	7/27/07	D. Bloomburg	3984	Warehouse

②

Material #	Material Description	Quantity
ENSB3000	Entry-Level Skateboard	50
HLMT5000	Helmet	10
SHRT4000	T-Shirt	10
FAID6000	Skateboard First-aid Kits	20

③

For use by Purchasing					
PO Date	Vendor	Requested Date	Delivery Location	F.O.B. POINT	TERMS
7/11/07	Black Widow Skateboards, Inc.	July 27, 2007	Warehouse	Destination	Net 30

④

Requisitioned by:	Name D. Bloomburg	Signature	Date: 7/9/07
PO created by:	Name M. SEWARD	Signature	Date: 7/11/07

Figure 3.2 Purchase requisition

In our example, when Martha receives the requisition, she selects Black Widow Skateboards, Inc. as the supplier (area 1 in Figure 3.3). She indicates that the materials are to be delivered to David's attention in the warehouse (area 1) and that the materials are to be *shipped via* ground shipment (area 2); that is, by means of a truck or similar vehicle. (Other options include shipment via air and train.) The purchase order also includes the *FOB point* as the "destination" and *payment terms* as "Net 30."

The **free-on-board (FOB)** point is the point at which ownership of the material in the shipment legally transfers from one company to the other. Typical FOB points are the *shipping point* and the *destination* (or *receiving point*). Why must the FOB be specified? The FOB point has major implications in the case of loss or damage to

Super Skateboard Builders, Inc.

1 Skateboard Drive
Grand Rapids, MI, 49525
Phone: 616.555.1234 Fax: 616.555.2234

PURCHASE ORDER

Purchase Order Number: 1546

THE PURCHASE ORDER NUMBER MUST APPEAR ON ALL RELATED CORRESPONDENCE, SHIPPING PAPERS, AND INVOICES

TO:
Black Widow Skateboards, Inc
1 Spider Way
Holland, MI, 49424
616.555.7834

SHIP TO:
Mr. David Bloomburg
SSB, Inc.
1 Skateboard Drive
Grand Rapids, MI, 49525
616.555.1234

Purchase Order #	P.O. DATE	Delivery Date	Shipped VIA	F.O.B. Point	Payment Terms
1546	July 11, 2007	July 27, 2007	Ground	Destination	Net 30

Quantity	Material #	Material Description	Unit Type	Unit Price	Item Total
50	ENSB3000	Entry-Level Skateboard	Each	34.00	1,700.00
10	HLMT5000	Helmet	Each	20.00	200.00
10	SHRT4000	T-Shirt	Each	7.00	70.00
20	FAID6000	Skateboard First-aid Kits	Each	10.00	200.00

SUBTOTAL	$ 2,170.00
SALES TAX	Exempt
SHIPPING & HANDLING	Included
OTHER	N/A
ORDER TOTAL	$ 2,170.00

Authorized by: _M. Seward, Purchasing Manager_

Date 7/11/07

Figure 3.3 Purchase order

the material when the shipment is in transit between the seller and buyer. If the FOB point is the shipping point, then the loss is borne by the buyer, because ownership changes to the buyer as soon as the shipment is sent. Conversely, if the FOB point is the destination, then the loss is borne by the sender, because ownership does not change until the material has been delivered.

Payment terms define how the company is to pay the vendor. In most cases payment is due either the date the company receives the invoice or the date it receives the shipment, whichever is later. If the company fails to make payment within the specified terms, then the supplier might add a finance charge. Typical payment terms include:

- Net nn, where nn specifies the number of days within which payment for the full amount of the invoice is due. In Figure 3.3, for example, the specified terms are Net 30, meaning that full payment is due within 30 days.

- X% mm/ Net nn, where × is a discount expressed as a percent of the total invoice amount. The company receives this discount if it makes payment within mm days. If it does not, then payment in full is due within nn days. For example, if the terms are 1% 10/Net 30, then payment is due in 30 days, but the company can take a discount of 1% if it sends the payment within 10 days.

The purchase order also includes details of the materials being ordered, along with the cost of the order (area 3). The unit type, also called the *unit of measure*, identifies the basic unit by which the material is counted or defined. Common examples are gallons, yards, and ounces. When material is counted in individual units, "each" is the unit of measure. Such material could also be counted by the dozen, box, carton, or pallet. *Unit price* is the price or cost of one unit (i.e., box, gallon, yard) of the material. *Item total*, also called line-item total, is the cost of the specified quantity of the material on each line. It is the unit cost multiplied by the quantity ordered. Finally, the *order total* is the sum total of all the item totals plus any taxes, shipping, and other charges.

Finally, Martha signs off on the purchase order, authorizing the purchase (area 4). At this time, she retrieves the requisition and adds the purchase order number (areas 5 in Figure 3.2), details about the vendor, and delivery and payment terms (area 3). She then signs the requisition to indicate that a purchase order has been created (area 4).

Martha then sends the purchase order to the vendor, Black Widow Skateboard, Inc. She files one copy for her records and sends a copy to the warehouse and one to the accounting department for use later in the process.

In our example one purchase order is created for one requisition. We adopted this approach to keep the process as simple as possible. In the real world of B2B, however, other options are possible. The purchasing department receives many requisitions daily from different people in the organization for a variety of materials. Sometimes it combines many requisitions to create one purchase order for the same vendor. One reason for consolidating requisitions is to take advantage of *quantity discounts*, which are price reductions that suppliers offer when customers purchase large quantities of materials. In other cases, it makes sense to purchase materials from different suppliers. In this case, one requisition may generate multiple purchase orders.

Packing List

When the vendor sends the shipment, a **packing list** (Figure 3.4), or delivery document, will accompany it. A packing list provides details about the materials contained in the shipment. It includes data about the purchase order for the shipment, the dates when the order was filled (packed) and shipped, and the persons involved in preparing the order. Finally, it includes details of the items contained

Figure 3.4 Vendor packing list

in the shipment, including quantities and weights. A packing list typically does not contain any pricing information. Rather, it identifies the contents of the shipment and allows one to verify that the material in the shipment matches the quantity and materials that were originally ordered.

In our example, the packing list identifies Black Widow Skateboards as the vendor (area 1 in Figure 3.4) and the destination of the shipment (area 3). It provides many details about the shipment (area 2), such as dates and the people at Black Widow who were involved with preparing (packing and checking) the shipment. It also indicates that the order was shipped via UPS ground, as requested in the purchase order. In addition, it provides SSB's (the customer) purchase order number as a reference so that when SSB receives the shipment, it can match it to a purchase order. It also specifies an *order number*, which is a unique identifying number assigned by the vendor that enables the vendor to track the status of the order in the vendor's organization. Similarly, the *customer number* uniquely identifies SSB as one of their customers. Both the order number and customer number are useful in case the customer requests information about the order.

The final section of the packing list (area 4) provides details of the items in the shipment. The *order quantity* is the quantity of each material ordered. This should be the same quantity specified in the purchase order. The *ship quantity* is the quantity of each material that was actually included in this shipment. Ideally, the ship quantity is the same as the order quantity. Sometimes, however, there are not enough materials in inventory. When this happens, the vendor can either wait until there are sufficient materials to ship the entire order or ship what is currently available and send the rest later. In the latter case the quantity that is to be shipped at a later date is known as the *backordered quantity*. Finally, the weight of the materials in the shipment and the total weight are included and are useful in calculating shipping charges. They also let the warehouse know how heavy the shipment is so that a suitable method of moving the materials can be used (e.g., forklift).

In our example, the packing list indicates that all four of the materials in the customer purchase order have been shipped, with nothing backordered. The shipment weighs a total of 462.50 pounds.

Goods Receipt Document

When the shipment arrives in the SSB warehouse, Tim Jones receives the shipment. He uses the customer purchase order number in the packing list (area 2) to retrieve a copy of the purchase order that SSB sent to Black Widow Skateboard. He then creates a **goods receipt document** (Figure 3.5), which verifies that the specified goods have been received. The goods receipt document contains a *goods receipt number* (area 1) that uniquely identifies the document. It also includes the date of the receipt and the name of the supplier (area 2). Like the packing list it includes the purchase order number associated with the receipt, and it specifies which products were ordered (area 3) along with the quantities ordered, received, and backordered. Finally, a signature (area 4) identifies the person receiving and verifying the goods.

In our example, Tim has received the goods and has verified that the ordered quantities are fully delivered, with no backorders. He sends the goods receipt document to the accounting department for later processing. He also files a copy of the document along with the corresponding purchase order and packing list.

In the unfortunate event of damaged, incorrect, or incomplete shipments, Tim must then initiate a **returns process** with the vendor. The returns process involves physically shipping any damaged, incorrect, or incomplete products back to the vendor and verifying that the vendor sends a replacement shipment. The returns process is very unpleasant for both the purchasing company and the vendor. It produces unwanted delays and extra effort for both parties. To avoid these problems, companies implement very detailed quality-control processes to verify that what is shipped is exactly what was ordered, what is received is what was ordered, and everything in the shipment is in the right condition for use in subsequent processes. Fortunately, quality control generally is effective. Consequently, the return process occurs infrequently in most industries, to the relief of both customers and vendors.

Vendor Invoice

Once the shipment is sent, the vendor will send an **invoice** (Figure 3.6), or bill, for the material shipped. The invoice is sent to accounting for payment. Accounting will

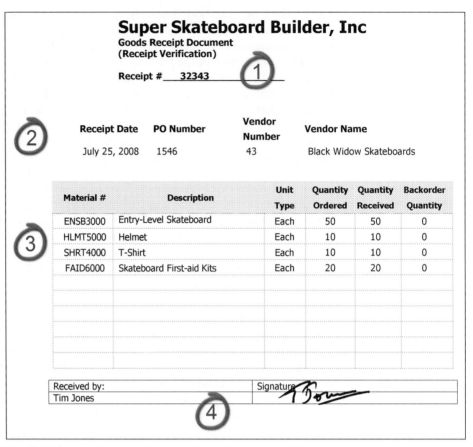

Figure 3.5 A goods receipt document

retrieve the corresponding purchase order and goods receipt (receipt verification) document and compare them to the invoice. If the data in all three documents match, a payment is sent to the vendor. This is called a **three-way match**. If the goods receipt document is not available, indicating that the shipment has not been received, then the invoice is filed with the purchase order. The customer does not send payment until it actually receives the goods and a three-way match is possible.

An invoice will identify the sender, the invoice number, invoice date, and recipient (area 1), plus the customer purchase order number and vendor order number and the terms of the order (area 2). Also included are the details of what the invoice is for, along with a total balance due (area 3). Finally, it provides information about who should be paid ("make checks payable to") and where to send payment (area 4).

Vendor Payment
When the three-way match has been achieved, the company makes a payment to the vendor. A variety of payment methods are possible. Generally, however, companies pay invoices either by check or electronic funds transfer, because both of these systems leave an obvious *paper trail*, or documented record of payment. SSB makes

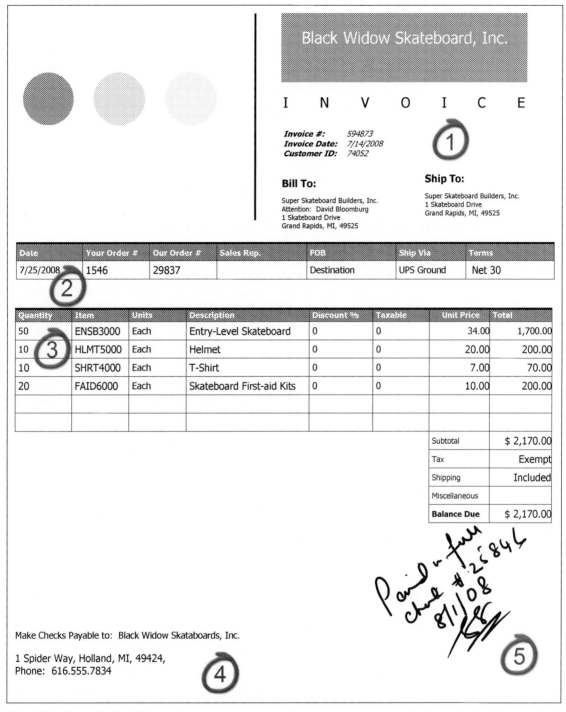

Figure 3.6 A vendor invoice

payment by check. Shana prepares and mails the check to the vendor and simply notes the details of the payment on the invoice (area 5). She then files the matching purchase order, goods receipt document, and invoice associated with the order. The order is now complete.

3.2.3 Information Flow

The third "flow" associated with a process is the information flow. Recall from Chapter 1 that the data generated in each step in the process are accumulated and organized in a manner that provides meaningful information about the process. This occurs at both the instance level of the process (relating to one execution of the procurement process) and at the aggregate or process level (relating to multiple instances of the process over time).

Instance-Level Information

Much of the instance-level information is related to the status of one particular instance of the process, that is, a specific purchase requisition. Status information is concerned with the state of the order as the process is executed. Has a purchase order been issued for a requisition? Have the goods been received? When were they received? Has an invoice been received and paid?

How do companies obtain the information they need to answer these questions? As we saw in Chapter 1, in a manual environment, this information is contained in and conveyed via the various paper documents discussed earlier. Companies obtain answers to these and other questions by manually retrieving and inspecting the appropriate documents, which is very time consuming and prone to inaccuracies.

Consider the instance of a procurement process discussed earlier. David wants to know the disposition of the purchase requisition he sent to Martha in purchasing. David must call Martha in purchasing for an answer. He does so and provides her with the requisition number. To determine if the requisition has a corresponding purchase order, Martha will retrieve a copy of the requisition from her files. If the requisition includes a purchase order number (area 5, in Figure 3.2), then Mary can provide David with the number. What if a purchase order number does not exist, however? In that case, two possibilities exist. The first is that Martha has not yet created the purchase order. The other is that she created an order but failed to note it on the requisition.

Suppose the vendor who supplied the materials calls David to see why his company has not been paid. David has to tell the vendor that he will get back to them with information about the payment. He then calls Shana to ask if payment was made for Black Widow Skateboards, and he provides the purchase order number. Shana retrieves her file for Black Widow Skateboards and finds the purchase order along with a goods receipt document and invoice. She notes that payment was made, and she provides David with the details, which he will then forward to the vendor. Consider an alternative scenario in which Shana has the purchase order and invoice but no goods receipt document. She therefore informs David that she is waiting for the goods to be delivered and for verification to be sent to her. David is now wondering why the vendor called for payment if the goods have not been delivered. He retrieves the purchase order from his files to see if there is a corresponding goods receipt document. To his surprise, he finds one. He now realizes that the problem is that Tim failed to send a copy to Shana, perhaps because he was extremely busy the day the materials were received.

Recall from Chapter 1 that activities between and among the various steps in a process must be carefully coordinated for the process to function efficiently and effectively. In a manual environment, this coordination is critically dependent on the efficient processing of the various documents. Unfortunately, processing documents manually tends to be inefficient and creates problems for the organization. For example, does a missing document indicate that a step has yet to be completed or that the paperwork has been incorrectly created, communicated, or filed? Companies waste substantial time and effort in clarifying such problems, and significant delays begin to accumulate between the various process steps.

Process-Level Information

Process-level information is concerned with the purchasing process on an overall level, across multiple instances (or requisitions). The company uses this information to understand how well it is executing each step in the process as well as how the entire process is operating over time. Data generated in the process must be aggregated over a certain time period (weekly, monthly, or quarterly) and converted into information. In the case of SSB, the following information is critical:

1. Which suppliers are prompt, and which ones are habitually late in delivering the materials ordered?
2. Which materials does SSB purchase most frequently, and from which suppliers?
3. What is the average time between sending a purchase order and receiving the materials? What is this average for each vendor? For each material?

Obtaining this information in a manual environment is quite difficult and time consuming because the data must be retrieved from a large number of documents and then formatted as information. Even with the use of productivity tools such as spreadsheets, this is a protracted task and is prone to frequent human errors.

3.2.4 Financial Impact

Some of the steps in the procurement process have an impact on the organization's financial position. Recall from Chapter 1 that a financial impact occurs when there is an exchange in value. In the simple procurement process illustrated in Figure 3.1, there is no exchange in value until the shipment is received from the vendor. The requisition is simply a request from individuals in the organization. Although a purchase order constitutes a financial obligation, the company incurs a debt only when it receives the shipment (more specifically, when ownership of the goods is transferred, as per the FOB terms). At this point, there is an increase in the value of inventory and in accounts payable, both of which are balance sheet accounts. Figure 3.7 shows the financial impact of the process used in our example. In Figure 3.7A, note that the value of both the finished goods inventory and accounts payable increased by $2170. Later, after the company has paid the vendor, both accounts payable and SSB's bank account will decrease by $2170 (Figure 3.7B).

▶ 3.3 ROLE OF ENTERPRISE SYSTEMS IN THE PROCUREMENT PROCESS

In Chapter 1 we explained that enterprise systems play an important role in enabling processes by (1) supporting the execution of the process, (2) capturing and storing the data generated by the process steps, and (3) helping the company monitor the performance of the process by providing instance-level and process-level information. Here we revisit this topic by focusing specifically on how a company can use an enterprise system to make its procurement process more efficient and productive.

```
┌─────────────────────────────────────────────────────────────────────┐
│ Figure A: When shipment is received from the vendor                   │
│ ┌───────────────────────────────┬───────────────────────────────────┐ │
│ │      Income Statement         │          Balance Sheet            │ │
│ │ Income                        │                                   │ │
│ │         Revenue from Sales    │  Assets                           │ │
│ │                               │          Bank Account             │ │
│ │                               │          Accounts Receivable      │ │
│ │ Expenses                      │          Inventory                │ │
│ │         Cost of Goods Sold    │              Finished goods ↑+$2170│ │
│ │                               │                                   │ │
│ │                               │  Total Assets          +$2170     │ │
│ │ Net Income                    │                                   │ │
│ │                               │  Liabilities                      │ │
│ │                               │          Accounts Payable ↑+$2170 │ │
│ │                               │                                   │ │
│ │                               │  Equity                           │ │
│ │                               │          Retained Earnings        │ │
│ │                               │                                   │ │
│ │                               │  Total Liabilities and Equity +$2170│ │
│ └───────────────────────────────┴───────────────────────────────────┘ │
│ Figure B: When payment is made to the vendor                          │
│ ┌───────────────────────────────┬───────────────────────────────────┐ │
│ │      Income Statement         │          Balance Sheet            │ │
│ │ Income                        │                                   │ │
│ │         Revenue from Sales    │  Assets                           │ │
│ │                               │          Bank Account       -$2170│ │
│ │                               │          Accounts Receivable      │ │
│ │ Expenses                      │          Inventory                │ │
│ │         Cost of Goods Sold    │              Finished goods +$2170│ │
│ │                               │                                   │ │
│ │                               │  Total Assets              $0     │ │
│ │ Net Income                    │                                   │ │
│ │                               │  Liabilities                      │ │
│ │                               │          Accounts Payable   ↓  $0 │ │
│ │                               │                                   │ │
│ │                               │  Equity                           │ │
│ │                               │          Retained Earnings        │ │
│ │                               │                                   │ │
│ │                               │  Total Liabilities and Equity  $0 │ │
│ └───────────────────────────────┴───────────────────────────────────┘ │
└─────────────────────────────────────────────────────────────────────┘
```

Figure 3.7 Financial impact of the procurement process

3.3.1 Execute the Process

Enterprise systems support the execution of processes in a number of ways. First, the needed documents can be quickly and easily created and stored in the system. This activity becomes even quicker and easier if the company automatically fills in some of the necessary data from previous steps, thus eliminating the need for employees to enter and reenter the same data over and over again. A fundamental feature of an ES is that all the relevant data and documents are stored in a common database. This arrangement makes it very easy for everybody involved in the process to quickly and easily retrieve the documents and data they need to complete their tasks. Second, communicating information between and among people in the organization can be automated. For example, after a purchase requisition is created, a notification can be automatically sent to the purchasing department. In these ways an ES can enable workers to complete their tasks both more quickly and more accurately than they can through manual processing. Figure 3.8 illustrates how the employees of SSB use

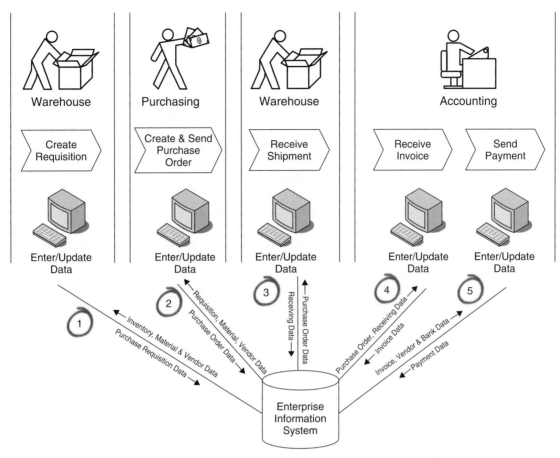

Figure 3.8 Enterprise system in the procurement process

their enterprise system to execute the procurement process. We refer to this figure throughout the following discussion.

Create Purchase Requisition

An enterprise system makes the task of creating a requisition much less complicated by providing easy access to the necessary data and by generating an online form that the user can complete. Some of the data on the form, such as dates, will be prepopulated. In addition, the system will allow the user to search for material numbers and will retrieve data about the materials, such as descriptions, that are necessary to complete the requisition. The user can also retrieve data about previous purchases. Finally, the user can request a specific supplier based on the supplier's past performance with the company.

In the case of SSB, David is responsible for maintaining a sufficient quantity of materials in inventory. Recall that in the manual environment David must rely on physical observations that the quantity of materials in the warehouse is getting low. With an ES, however, David can simply retrieve an inventory report from the system to determine if a requisition is necessary (see area 1 in Figure 3.8). Moreover, as Figure 3.8 illustrates, the ES also provides David with other data he will need, such as vendors and purchasing history.

Based on the data he has retrieved from the system, David has determined that inventory is getting low and therefore a requisition is necessary. He accesses the program to create a requisition, which displays a form that must be completed (Figure 3.9). David searches for and includes the four materials he wishes to purchase (Figure 3.9, area 1). He also includes the desired quantities, delivery date, and delivery location. The system automatically includes the description of the materials. In addition, at David's request, the system has provided some historical data about previous purchases (area 2). The data indicate that SSB has previously purchased entry-level skateboards from four vendors for a price of $34 each. When David saves the requisition, the system will add a unique requisition number and will note the current date and the name of the individual (David) who created the requisition. This requisition is stored in the common system database (Figure 3.8, area 1) and is immediately accessible to other workers in the organization as they complete the subsequent steps in the process.

In our example, David uses the system to access an inventory report to determine if more materials must be ordered and then creates a requisition himself. However, SSB could configure the system to notify David automatically via e-mail that the quantity in stock has dropped below some predetermined level. David could then create the requisition in the system. Going further, in highly automated

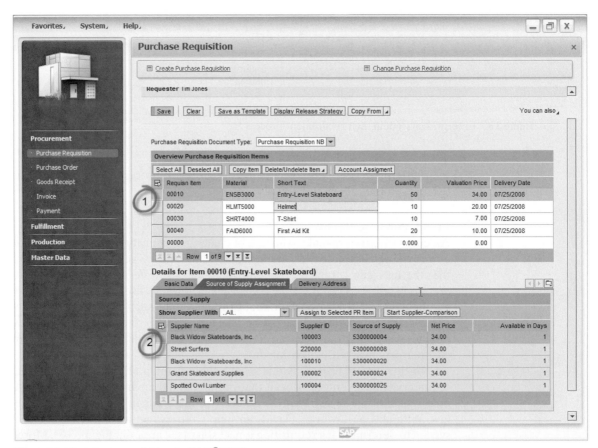

Figure 3.9 Purchase requisition in SAP® ERP
Source: Copyright SAP AG 2008

environments the system not only can determine that materials must be ordered, but it can generate the requisition itself.

Create Purchase Order

How does Martha, the purchasing manager, know that there are requisitions that need her attention? In a manual environment, she receives the paper requisition via interoffice mail. In contrast, with an enterprise system, Martha has access to all the data she needs. She simply logs into the system and retrieves a list of pending requisitions (Figure 3.8 area 2). Also, like David, Martha also has access to other data she needs, such as vendors and previous purchases.

Once Martha has determined that there are requisitions she must act on, she will access the program to create a purchase order (Figure 3.10). The program will also display the requisitions (area 1). Note that there are requisitions for entry-level skateboards, first aid kit, helmets, and T-shirts, for a total of four items. She chooses to process all four of these items and transfers them into the purchase order (area 2). She selects Black Widow Skateboards as the supplier (area 3). The system automatically transfers all the necessary data from the requisition into the purchase order. In addition, it includes pricing for each of the products as well as taxes and shipping charges. It then calculates the total cost of the order. Finally, the system will add a unique purchase order number and note that Martha is the person who created the PO. When Martha is satisfied with the order, the system will save the data in the common database (Figure 3.8 area 2).

In our example, Martha queried the system to determine if there are requisitions to process, just as David accessed the system to determine whether he needed to order more materials. As was true with David, however, SSB could have configured the system to notify Martha via e-mail when requisitions are created. In highly automated environments, the system can automatically generate purchase orders and either electronically dispatch them to the vendors or await a final approval from the purchasing manager.

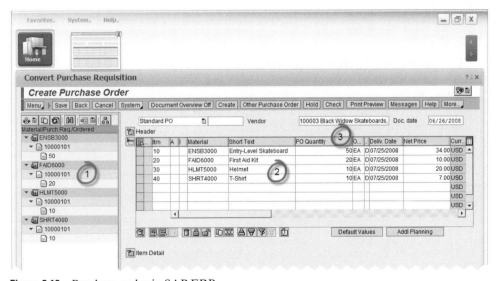

Figure 3.10 Purchase order in SAP ERP
Source: Copyright SAP AG 2008

Receive Shipment

Recall that when a shipment arrives from a vendor, it is accompanied by a packing list. The packing list identifies the contents of the shipment. It also includes the purchase order number associated with the shipment. In the manual environment, Tim must find the matching purchase order in his files. In contrast, with an enterprise system these data can be easily accessed from the common database (Figure 3.8 area 3).

When Tim receives the shipment in the warehouse, he will log into the system to record the receipt of the materials. He will access the program to create a goods receipt (Figure 3.11). He will provide the system with the purchase order number (area 1), and the system will retrieve the materials and quantities in that purchase order (area 2). Tim will verify that the quantities in the shipment match those on the goods receipt document. If they don't, then he will record the actual quantities received. In addition, he will note the location in the warehouse where he has stored the materials (area 3). He will then save the data, at which point the system will assign a unique number to the goods receipt document and will note that Tim was the person who created the document. These data are stored in the system database (Figure 3.8 area 3)

Receive Invoice and Send Payment

Within a few days of sending the shipment to the customer, the vendor will typically send an invoice. In a manual environment, Shana, SSB's accountant, must retrieve the purchase order and goods receipt document from her files and match them with the data in the invoice. An ES makes it easier for her to access these documents and match them with the invoice (Figure 3.8 area 4).

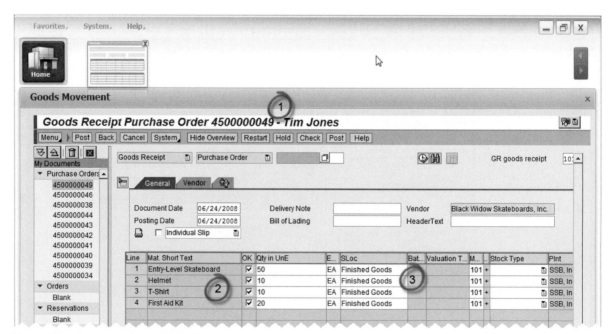

Figure 3.11   Goods receipt in SAP ERP

Source: Copyright SAP AG 2008

How does Shana utilize the ES to assist with these tasks? First, she logs into the system and accesses the transaction to create and verify an invoice (Figure 3.12). She then provides the invoice amount (area 1) and the purchase order number (area 2). At this point the system retrieves and displays the vendor information (area 3) and the materials, quantities, and cost (area 4). The invoice amount that Shana entered (area 1) must match the total of the items in the purchase order (area 4). When Shana is satisfied, she saves the invoice. The system then assigns the invoice a unique number and notes that Martha recorded the invoice. Finally, these data are placed back into the system database (Figure 3.8 area 4).

Notice that the ES performs the three-way match automatically. The system already has the purchase order and goods receipt data from the previous steps. When Shana adds the invoice data, the system completes the three-way match without the need for anybody to physically compare papers, as is done in the manual process. In addition, the system can also verify whether the invoice (1) has already been paid, (2) contains the correct discounts from special payment terms (e.g., 1%10/Net 30), and (3) has open items that require special attention. By performing these tasks the

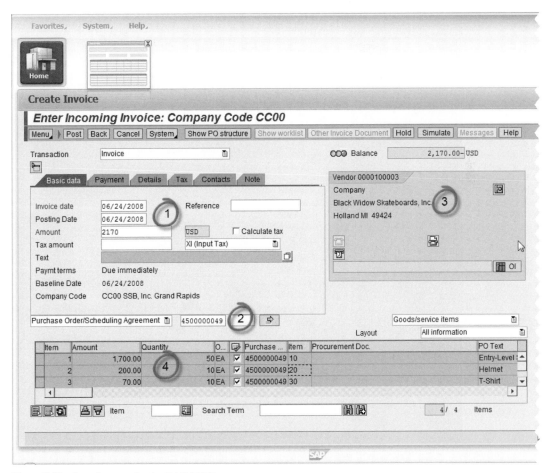

Figure 3.12 Invoice receipt in SAP ERP
Source: Copyright SAP AG 2008

ES significantly reduces the manual workload of the accounting department and allows them to focus on higher-value activities.

Finally, Shana will make a payment to Black Widow Skateboards. Figure 3.8 (area 5) illustrates that the ES provides her with the data she needs to process this payment. The resulting payment data are placed back in the system database.

Shana will log into the system and access the program to process vendor payments (Figure 3.13A). She will provide the bank account number and amount of payment (area 1), and the vendor number (area 2). In turn, the system will display the vendor name (Figure 3.13B, area 1) and any open invoices for that vendor (Figure 3.13B, area 2). Shana notes that the amount of the payment matches the amount of the invoices, and she saves the data. Depending on how the system is configured, the system either will electronically transfer funds from SSB's bank account to the vendor's bank account, or Shana will prepare a check and mail it to Black Widow Skateboards.

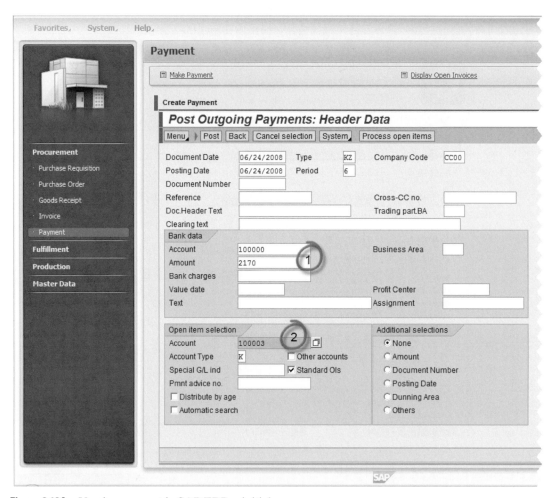

Figure 3.13A   Vendor payment in SAP ERP—initial screen
Source: Copyright SAP AG 2008

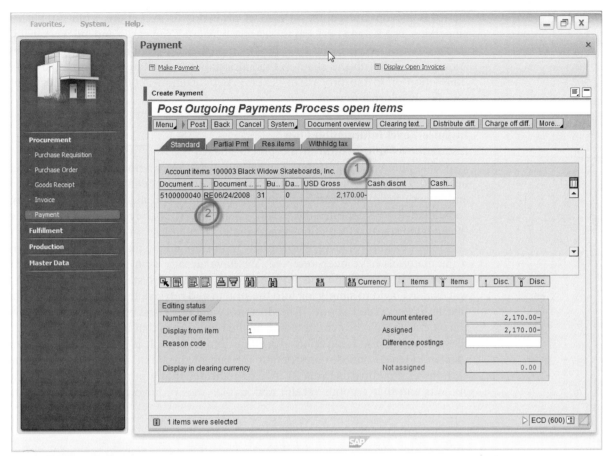

Figure 3.13B Vendor payment in SAP ERP—processing
Source: Copyright SAP AG 2008

3.3.2 Capture and Store Process Data

In addition to helping a company execute the process, an ES efficiently captures and stores data associated with the process. We have already seen that, as each step of the process is completed, the relevant data—vendor's name, quantity ordered, purchase order number, and so on—are automatically saved in the system, where other people involved in the process can access them. Some of these data, such as dates and the identity of the person completing the task, are automatically captured by the system. Other data, such as material numbers, quantities, and prices, are either accessed from the database (having been stored there during a previous step) or entered by the user. In either case, these data not only speed up the process, but they are also invaluable in monitoring the process to ensure everything is running as efficiently as possible. We discuss the role of the ES in monitoring the process in the next section.

3.3.3 Monitor the Process

Enterprise systems provide the information needed to monitor the state of a process. In many cases the ES can be configured to automatically monitor the process and alert the appropriate people in case of problems or **exceptions** from established guidelines. The ES can perform these tasks because it can easily and quickly retrieve **status information**, provide a variety of reports, and respond to specific queries. As we saw earlier in the chapter, this information can relate either to a particular transaction or to the process in general. Let's examine both cases as they apply specifically to procurement.

Instance-Level Information Flow

Instance-level information in the procurement process is related to the status of a specific purchase requisition. Typical questions are whether the requisition has been acted on and, if so, whether the purchase order has been created, the shipment and invoice have been received, and payment has been made. As these steps are completed, the ES captures these data. Therefore, when the requisition is retrieved, the updated status information is immediately available.

In our example, David, who initially requisitioned the materials, wants to know if the materials have been received. We have already seen how difficult and time consuming it is to obtain this information in a manual system. In contrast, an ES will enable David to simply log into the system and retrieve the purchase requisition that he is concerned about. If he does not remember the requisition number, he can quickly search the system to find all the requisitions that he created. Figure 3.14 shows the purchase requisition with status information. It identifies the requisition number (area 1) and displays details for one of the items in the requisition, the entry-level skateboards (area 2). Area 3 indicates that a purchase order exists for 50 units and that a goods receipt and invoice receipt have been recorded for the

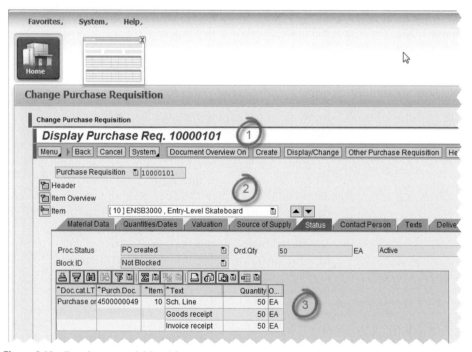

Figure 3.14   Purchase requisition history
Source: Copyright SAP AG 2008

50 units. If David wants more details, he will click on the purchase order number (area 3), and the system will display the purchase order history (Figure 3.15).

The purchase order history indicates that Martha created the purchase order (area 1), and it provides the goods receipt and invoice receipt numbers (area 2). Clicking on these numbers will provide David with details, such as who completed the steps and when. This ability to **drill down** into details is a very powerful capability of enterprise systems. An ES has this capability because all the data are stored in a common database and therefore can be accessed as and when they are needed.

This information about the status of a process is used to determine if the current state is acceptable or if there is a problem. The current state is measured against a standard definition of what is expected, or **key performance indicators** (KPI). For example, if the KPI for acting on a requisition is five days and if the status report does not show a purchase order after six days, then there is a problem with the execution of the process, and an exception has occurred. The company must then decide how to handle this exception. They might conclude that manual intervention—for example phoning Martha to investigate the cause of the delay—is the best strategy. Similarly, if a goods receipt is not indicated on the status section of a requisition or the purchase order within the standard number of days, then an exception has occurred. In this case a call to Tim in the warehouse may be in order to see if the shipment has arrived and is waiting to be received. If the shipment has not arrived, then the company needs to call the vendor to determine the cause of the delay.

In highly automated environments, the ES can be configured to perform some of this monitoring automatically. For example, if the requisition has not been acted on within the standard number of days, the ES can send an e-mail alert to both David and Martha. Similarly, if a shipment is not received within an expected period of time, the system can automatically send an e-mail reminder or inquiry to the vendor.

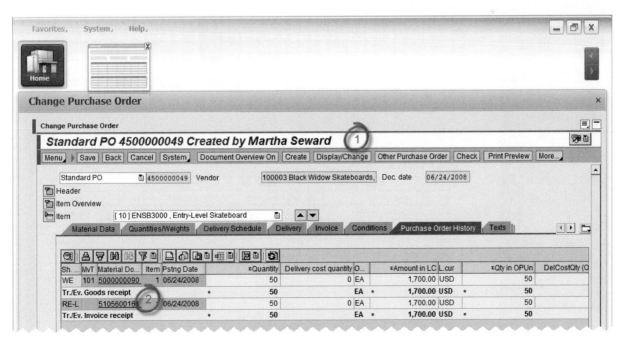

Figure 3.15   Purchase order history
Source: Copyright SAP AG 2008

Process-Level Information Flow

We now conclude our discussion by explaining how an ES can help monitor the procurement process as a whole. The document reproduced in Figure 3.16 provides information about the procurement process for the entire month of January. It shows a summary for the month (area 1) that indicates a total of seven purchases averaging nearly $3000 per order. Details of each order are provided at the bottom part of the figure (area 2). Included here are the order number, vendor name, materials purchased, order date, total amount of the order, and the current status of the order. The "Status" column indicates that there are currently two new orders, two that have been delivered by the vendor, and one that has been partially delivered. In addition, one order is still being processed by the vendor, and one was cancelled by the company after it initially sent the purchase order to the vendor. Double-clicking on a specific order will display the purchase order and all the data associated with the order. In the top right part of the figure, a bar chart summarizes the total value of purchases for each vendor. For instance, the bar chart indicates that our company purchased the most materials, in terms of value of the orders, from Grand Skateboard Suppliers.

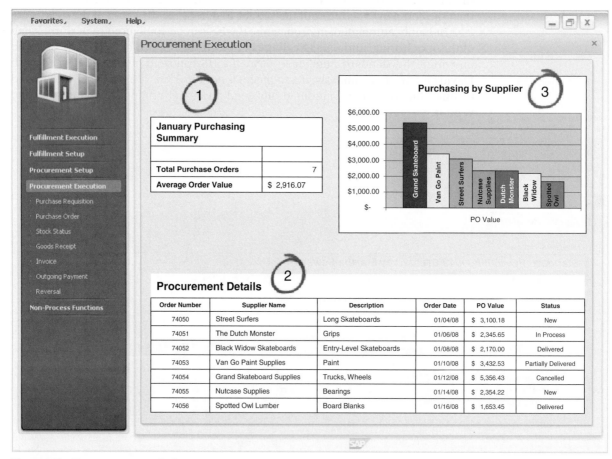

Figure 3.16   Procurement analytics
Source: Copyright SAP AG 2008

▶ 3.4 EXERCISE USING SIMULATED SAP ERP

So far we have discussed the procurement process in terms of the various flows—physical, data and document, and information. We have also explained how enterprise systems support the procurement process. It is now time for you to experience an enterprise system in action in the simulated SAP environment.

Go to WileyPLUS, and complete the exercises for this chapter. The exercises consist of three parts: two exercises—a guided practice exercise, and a second one that you must complete on your own without any guidance—and a short quiz.

The exercises will require you to complete the steps in the procurement process that have been discussed in this chapter. In particular you will

1. Create a purchase requisition for a number of trading goods
2. Convert the requisition to a purchase order
3. Enter a goods receipt into the system
4. Enter a vendor invoice into the system
5. Record a payment to the vendor

In the guided exercise, the system will purchase a number of materials from one of SSB's vendors. The system will guide you as to what you must do to complete each step of the process. The steps in the exercises mirror the steps explained in the chapter. We urge you to pay attention to what you are doing and to refer to the chapter as needed to fully understand the activities in the exercise.

In the second exercise, you will be asked to repeat the same steps for a different set of materials to be purchased from a different vendor. Unlike the first exercise, this one does not offer any guidance. Essentially, you are on your own. The simulation is designed so that you cannot make a mistake. The system will accept only correct actions from you before it proceeds to the next step! Once again, we urge you to understand what you are doing and why.

The final part of the exercise involves a short quiz, consisting of review questions. These review questions are designed to test your knowledge and understanding of procurement process and the related exercises. Your instructor will direct you to the location of the quiz. After you have completed the quiz, the system will grade it and send your score to your professor's grade book. You may view your score in the gradebook tab of WileyPLUS.

You may repeat these exercises as often as necessary to thoroughly understand the procurement process and how an ES supports it.

▶ CHAPTER SUMMARY

In this chapter we discussed a very simple procurement process that is used to acquire needed materials—raw materials, supplies, trading goods, and so forth. Purchasing in business-to-business commerce is significantly more complex than in a consumer context given the higher risk and higher value of the relationships between suppliers and customers. We limited the discussion to a few simple steps; however, procurement processes used in businesses are far more complex and differ greatly between companies and industries. Our purpose was to help you understand the fundamentals of the process in terms of the different flows—physical, data, document, and information.

A procurement process includes steps that must be completed in a particular order by people in different parts of the organization—purchasing, warehouse, and accounting. When a need for more materials arises, it is formalized using a purchase requisition. The requisition is then reviewed and a purchase order is created and sent to a suitable vendor. A purchase order represents a legal obligation to purchase the specified materials, for the specified price, under the terms laid out in the order. When a vendor sends a shipment, it is accompanied by a packing list that identifies the contents of the shipment. This is used to receive the materials in the warehouse and prepare a goods receipt document. When a vendor invoice is received by the accounting department, a three-way match involving the purchase order, goods receipt document, and the invoice leads to a payment.

Enterprise systems play a critical role in the execution of the procurement process and provide meaningful information needed to monitor the process. They facilitate communication and coordination of work between the different functional areas due to the tight integration between process steps and centrally managed data. Better coordination leads to increased process efficiency as tasks are completed faster and with fewer errors. Enterprise systems also eliminate a great deal of paperwork and time-consuming manual steps. This is particularly true in highly automated environments where the ability of the enterprise system to automatically manage and complete certain tasks is extremely powerful. The ultimate result is reduced lead times and cycle times, increased visibility, and a reduction in inventory.

► KEY TERMS

business-to-business (B2B) commerce
drill down
exceptions
free-on-board (FOB)

goods receipt document
invoice
key performance indicators
packing list

payment terms
procurement process
purchase order
purchase requisition
returns process

status information
three-way match

► REVIEW QUESTIONS

1. In what ways is business-to-consumer purchasing different from business-to-business purchasing?

2. Explain the key steps in a basic procurement process.

3. Briefly describe the key documents in the procurement process in terms of their role in the process.

4. Describe the three-way match in a manual system. Explain how it differs from the automated three-way match in an enterprise system.

5. Define the following terms:
   (a) Free-on-board
   (b) Payment terms
   (c) Quantity discount
   (d) Backordered quantity
   (e) Three-way match

► ASSIGNMENTS

1. The procurement process described in this chapter is deliberately very simple. Based on your experiences or by talking to someone in a local company, define and describe a more complex procurement process in terms of the physical, document and data flows. What functions of the organization will be involved in this process?

2. This chapter provides some examples of instance-level and process-level information. Identify two more examples of each type of information and explain what data will be needed to generate this information. What is the source of these data?

3. Identify some of the key problems associated with the manual, or paper-based, procurement process. How does an enterprise system eliminate or reduce the impact of these problems?

4. SSB has a need to purchase the following materials from its supplier, Black Widow Skateboards. Create all the documents used in the process to procure these materials. You can search the Internet for examples of the documents included in this chapter or you can create them using a word processor.

- 100 Entry-level skateboards
- 300 T-shirts
- 100 First aid kits

5. For the process in Question 4, explain the financial impact of the process steps on SSB. Draw a diagram similar to the figure used in this chapter to explain the financial impact.

CHAPTER 4

The Fulfillment Process

Learning Objectives

After completing this chapter you will be able to:

▶ Describe the steps in the fulfillment process.

▶ Explain the role of different functional areas in efficiently and effectively completing the fulfillment process.

▶ Identify the key steps in the fulfillment process and the data, document, and information flows associated with it.

▶ Explain the financial impact of the steps in the fulfillment process.

▶ Explain the role of enterprise systems in supporting the fulfillment process.

The previous chapter explained how SSB purchases, or procures, the products it plans to sell. This chapter will discuss the process through which SSB sells these products to its customers. We call this process the fulfillment process, also known as the *order-to-cash* process.

Recall that, for the time being, SSB does not manufacture its products in-house. Rather, it purchases these products from its suppliers and then resells them to its customers. As the company's owner, John needs to understand the process of filling customer orders. Specifically, he needs to learn what steps are involved, which documents are needed, and what data SSB should keep track of. His goal is to determine the most effective system for keeping track of customers' orders so that SSB can answer customers' questions about the status of their orders. He also wants to determine how well SSB's fulfillment process is working. Who are its best customers? Which products are selling well? Which are not? Is SSB receiving customer payments in a timely manner?

Recall from Chapter 1 that the fulfillment process includes all the steps necessary to take an order from a customer; fill, pack, and ship it; and receive payment for it. We begin our discussion by presenting a simple fulfillment process in terms of the data, document, and information flows. We then discuss the financial impact of the different steps in the process. Finally, we examine the role of enterprise systems (ES) in supporting the fulfillment process.

▶ 4.1 KEY CONCEPTS AND ASSUMPTIONS

The fulfillment process differs greatly depending on the countries, industries, and products that the company must deal with. A company can choose from several strategies for fulfillment. Two of the most common strategies are *sell-from-stock* and *configure-to-order*.

Sell-from-stock involves fulfilling customer orders directly from the company's inventory of finished goods. Basically, customers are limited to purchasing only those products that are in stock; they can't request special or customized products. Sell-from-stock is common among companies that sell directly to the consumer via retail. These tend to be high-volume, low-cost operations, such as grocery stores, office supply stores, and fashion retailers.

In contrast, **configure-to-order** usually involves taking a standard or base model of a product and then configuring it to meet the customer's special needs by adding either special options or add-on parts. The configure-to-order strategy is common in low-volume, high-cost industries that require specialized products that must meet very specific needs. For example, companies in the chemical and the petroleum industries use similar pumps and pipes, but use them for different purposes. Consequently, they must be configured differently to meet the unique needs of each customer. The configure-to-order fulfillment process requires suppliers and customers to collaborate closely to ensure that the customer's special needs are met.

The examples of the Apple iPod and Mac computer are used to illustrate the two fulfillment strategies in Business Processes in Practice 4-1.

▶ **BUSINESS PROCESSES IN PRACTICE 4-1**

APPLE iPOD AND MAC COMPUTERS

We have seen that the two major strategies companies use to fulfill customer orders are sell-from-stock and configure-to-order. Let's look at examples you are probably familiar with to see how these processes work in the real world. In some companies, such as Apple, both strategies may be used simultaneously for different products.

Most of you have either purchased an Apple iPod or knows someone who has iPods are relatively high-volume, low-cost products sold online and through retail outlets worldwide. When a customer wants to purchase an iPod through the Apple online store, she must choose which model she wants and perhaps also the color and/or style she prefers. She then goes to the checkout and submits her order. Apple takes her payment and processes the order. The warehouse picks the product from the storage location, packs it in a box, and ships it to the customer. This entire process is an example of sell-from-stock because Apple is selling a finished good (iPod) from its warehouse or in-store stock. Customers can only purchase an iPod that is in stock at that moment. Otherwise they have to wait until Apple manufactures more of that particular model. There are no options for customers to order a special iPod model that is not currently being manufactured or to request that Apple add special features to an existing model.

In contrast, a customer who wishes to purchase a Mac computer from the online Apple store goes through a different fulfillment process. A Mac computer is a lower-volume higher-cost product compared to an iPod. When customers select the basic model of the Mac they would like, they are presented with several options related to memory, hard disk size, additional software, and accessories. This is the configure-to-order fulfillment process. Apple manufactures a base model of each of its main Mac computers, stores them in the warehouse, and then custom-configures the final version according to each customer's requirements as reflected on the sales order. There are only a few options that customers can choose from, but even those few options create hundreds of potential configurations of the same base machine. Contrast this system with the iPod, where customers' choices are largely limited to the available models, colors, and styles, and custom-configuring isn't an option.

Note that both fulfillment processes start and end with the same basic steps. As you can see, however, the configure-to-order process requires a great deal more effort than the much simpler sell-from-stock process. Companies must determine which process works best depending on the types of products they are selling and the purchasing behavior of their customers. They must also determine if their company should support both processes at the same time for different product lines, as in Apple's case.

Source: Compiled from Apple company reports; "Back to the Future at Apple," *Business Week*, May 25, 1998; and "The build-to-order dilemma," *MacWorld*, May 1, 1998.

▶ 4.2 A BASIC FULFILLMENT PROCESS

As we explained at the beginning of the chapter, we start by presenting a simple fulfillment process to highlight the basic flows in the process. Figure 4.1 illustrates the functional areas in the organization that are involved in the process, the key steps in this process, and some of the documents associated with the process. The four flows associated with the process are discussed next. The steps depicted in the figure are highlighted in the explanation that follows.

4.2.1 Physical Flow

The fulfillment process often begins when a customer sends an inquiry regarding the availability of the products he intends to purchase. (See "*receive customer inquiry*" in Figure 4.1.) This inquiry is received by Matt Jones in the sales department, who then creates a quotation and sends it back to the customer. Next, the customer sends a purchase order to Matt ("*receive customer purchase order*"). When Matt receives this order, he creates a sales order and forwards it to Tim in the warehouse for further processing. Tim then prepares the shipment. He gathers the right quantities of the desired products from the storage shelves, puts them in a box, seals it, and places an address label on it. He then sends this box to the customer by some means, such as a truck or airline ("*send shipment*"). Next, Shana in accounting will prepare an invoice or bill and send it to the customer ("*create and send invoice*"). Hopefully the customer will send a payment, perhaps in the form of a check, which is received and recorded ("*receive payment*").

As in the procurement process, it is necessary to understand how the various people involved in the fulfillment process know when and how they need to complete their part in the process. How does Tim know to prepare a shipment? What will be contained in the shipment? How does Shana know when to send a bill to the customer? How does she know what was shipped to the customer and how much to charge? Recall that companies use various documents to communicate and share data across the different processes. In the next section, we next discuss the documents associated with the fulfillment process as well as the key data contained in these documents.

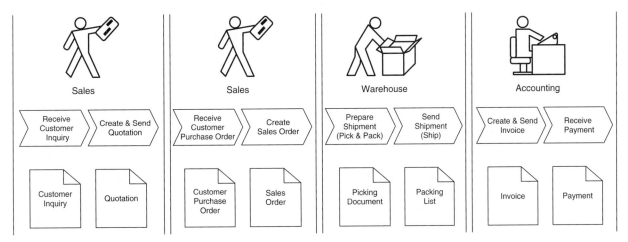

Figure 4.1 Simple fulfillment process

4.2.2 Document and Data Flow

Figure 4.1 also identifies some of the documents commonly found in a fulfillment process. The documents associated with the fulfillment process at SSB are:

1. Customer inquiry
2. Quotation
3. Customer purchase order
4. Sales order
5. Picking document
6. Packing list
7. Customer invoice
8. Customer payment

These documents and the key data in each are discussed below. A detailed explanation of the data is provided in the appendix.

Customer Inquiry

As we saw in the previous section, a **customer inquiry** (Figure 4.2) is a request for information about the *availability* and prices of the products specified in the inquiry.

World Wide Skateboard Distributors
1229 Westwinde Street
Ann Arbor, MI, 48109
Phone 734.555.5638 Fax 734.555.5648

Date: 6/2/08

To Whom It May Concern:

My name is Patrick Wilson, and I am a purchasing agent for World Wide Skateboard Distributors in Ann Arbor, MI. I was looking through your catalog, and I would like to receive a quote for the following items:

Quantity	Item	Material Number.
20	Skateboard first aid kit	FAID6000
10	SSB Inc. T-Shirt	SHRT4000
50	Entry-level skateboard	ENSB3000
10	Helmet	HLMT5000

A quote by email or fax would be ideal.
Thank you

Patrick Wilson
Purchasing Agent
Fax: (734) 555-5648

Figure 4.2 Customer inquiry

It includes data such as the customer (area 1 in Figure 4.2), the products the customer is interested in and the quantities desired (area 2), and the individual who actually sent the inquiry (area 3). The example in Figure 4.2 indicates that Patrick Wilson of World Wide Skateboard Distributors (hereafter abbreviated "World Wide"), an SSB customer located in Ann Arbor, Michigan, is inquiring about the availability and cost of 20 skateboard first aid kits, 10 T-shirts, 50 entry-level skateboards, and 10 helmets. This inquiry was sent via e-mail to SSB.

Quotation

After the sales department receives the inquiry, it prepares a **quotation** in response. A quotation spells out the availability and prices of the materials specified in the inquiry. In our example, Matt receives the inquiry and prepares the quotation displayed in Figure 4.3. The quotation is addressed to the person sending the inquiry, Patrick Wilson (area 1). It specifies a *validity period* of 30 days (area 2), meaning that the prices and availability listed in the quotation are guaranteed for that period of

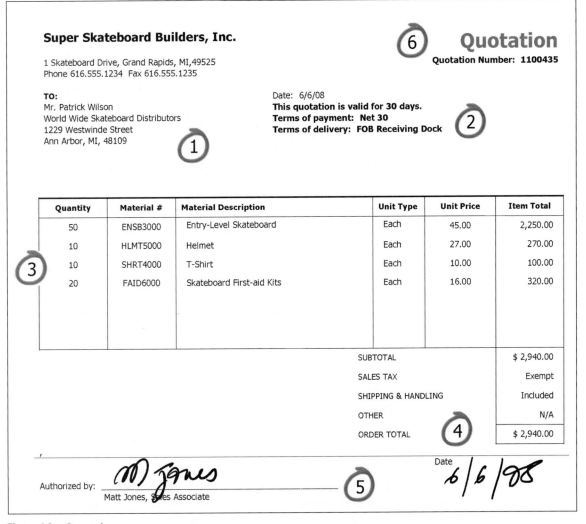

Figure 4.3 Quotation

time but not beyond that. Keep in mind that a quotation is based on the conditions that exist at the time the document is prepared. Specifying a validity period prevents a customer from attempting to use the quotation at a much later point in time, when conditions related to prices and availability may have changed. The quotation also includes *terms of payment* and delivery (area 2). Figure 4.3 specifies payment terms of "Net 30" and *delivery terms* of "FOB receiving dock." Terms of payment and delivery for the fulfillment process are the same as those for procurement, which we discussed in Chapter 3. A quotation also includes pricing per unit and for each line item (area 3) as well as a total for the entire order (area 4). SSB's quotation indicates a total of $2,940. Going further, the quotation provides the name of the person preparing the document, which in our example is Matt Jones (area 5). Finally, the quotation is identified by a unique *quotation number*—1100435—which is located at the top (area 6). This number is useful because it allows the quotation to be uniquely identified in case it must be retrieved to answer a customer's question or to verify that a potential customer order meets the terms of the quotation. The company sends the quotation to the customer by fax or e-mail and files a paper copy for its records.

Customer Purchase Order

After receiving the quotation, the customer must decide if the pricing and terms offered are satisfactory. If they are, then the customer communicates a desire to purchase the materials in the form of a **customer purchase order** (PO). A purchase order is an agreement to purchase the stated material, for the stated price, under the stated terms. Recall that we discussed purchase orders in Chapter 3 in the context of the procurement process. In the fulfillment process, the document is the same, but the data reflect the perspective of SSB's customer rather than SSB.

As illustrated in Figure 4.4, World Wide has sent a PO to SSB with a unique *PO number*—100074 (area 1)—for quantities and prices that match SSB's quotation (area 2). Area 3 identifies the terms of payment and delivery as well as the preferred *mode of shipment*. As was true of payment and delivery terms, the various shipment options we discussed in Chapter 3 are applicable here as well. In this case, World Wide has requested that the order be shipped via ground delivery to arrive by August 1. Finally, area 4 identifies the person authorizing the order, in this case Patrick Wilson.

Sales Order

When the company receives the customer PO, it creates an internal document called a **sales order** (Figure 4.5). In SSB, sales orders are also created in the sales department. Because the PO is based on the company's original quotation, it should contain the same information regarding the products, quantities, pricing, and delivery date that were on the quotation. Have you noticed that in each step of the process, from the customer inquiry to the quotation to the sales order, there has been a lot of repetition of this key information? You might suspect that this redundancy wastes valuable time and resources. In fact, repeating the essential information ensures that both the company and the customer share a clear understanding of the details related to the transaction.

A sales order serves two primary purposes. First, it standardizes data across all customer POs. Purchase orders from different customers are unlikely to have the same appearance in terms of content, format, and layout. A sales order contains all the necessary data in a format that is best suited to the organization receiving the

World Wide Skateboard Distributors

1229 Westwinde Street
Ann Arbor, MI, 48109
Phone 734.555.5638 Fax 734.555.55648

PURCHASE ORDER
Purchase Order Number: 100074

THE PURCHASE ORDER NUMBER MUST APPEAR ON ALL RELATED CORRESPONDENCE, SHIPPING DOCUMENTS, AND INVOICES

TO:
Mr. Matt Jones
SSB, Inc.
1 Skateboard Drive
Grand Rapids, MI, 49525
616.555.1234

SHIP TO:
World Wide Skateboard Distributors
Mid West Warehouse
1229 Westwinde Street
Ann Arbor, MI, 48109
Phone 734.555.5638 Fax 734.555.5648

Purchase Order #	P.O. DATE	Delivery Date	Shipped VIA	F.O.B. Point	Payment Terms
100074	July 15, 2008	August 1, 2008	Ground	Receiving Dock	Net 30

Quantity	Material #	Material Description	Unit Type	Unit Price	Item Total
50	ENSB3000	Entry-Level Skateboard	Each	45.00	2,250.00
10	HLMT5000	Helmet	Each	27.00	270.00
10	SHRT4000	T-Shirt	Each	10.00	100.00
20	FAID6000	Skateboard First-aid Kits	Each	16.00	320.00

SUBTOTAL	$ 2,940.00
SALES TAX	Exempt
SHIPPING & HANDLING	Included
OTHER	N/A
ORDER TOTAL	$ 2,940.00

Authorized by: _P. Wilson_
P. Wilson, Purchasing Agent

Date 7/15/08

Figure 4.4 Customer purchase order

order. It is easier to deal with a document (the sales order) that always looks the same and has the same data in the same place than to deal with customer purchase orders that vary in format and content.

A sales order will include relevant data from the customer PO such as name, address, and quantities. It also contains additional data needed to complete the process, such as the customer account number and an internal *sales order number*. This is a number assigned by the organization receiving the customer order. It is different from the customer PO number, which is assigned by the customer when it creates the PO. The sales order number is a key piece of data that is used to track the status of the order as it flows through the fulfillment process.

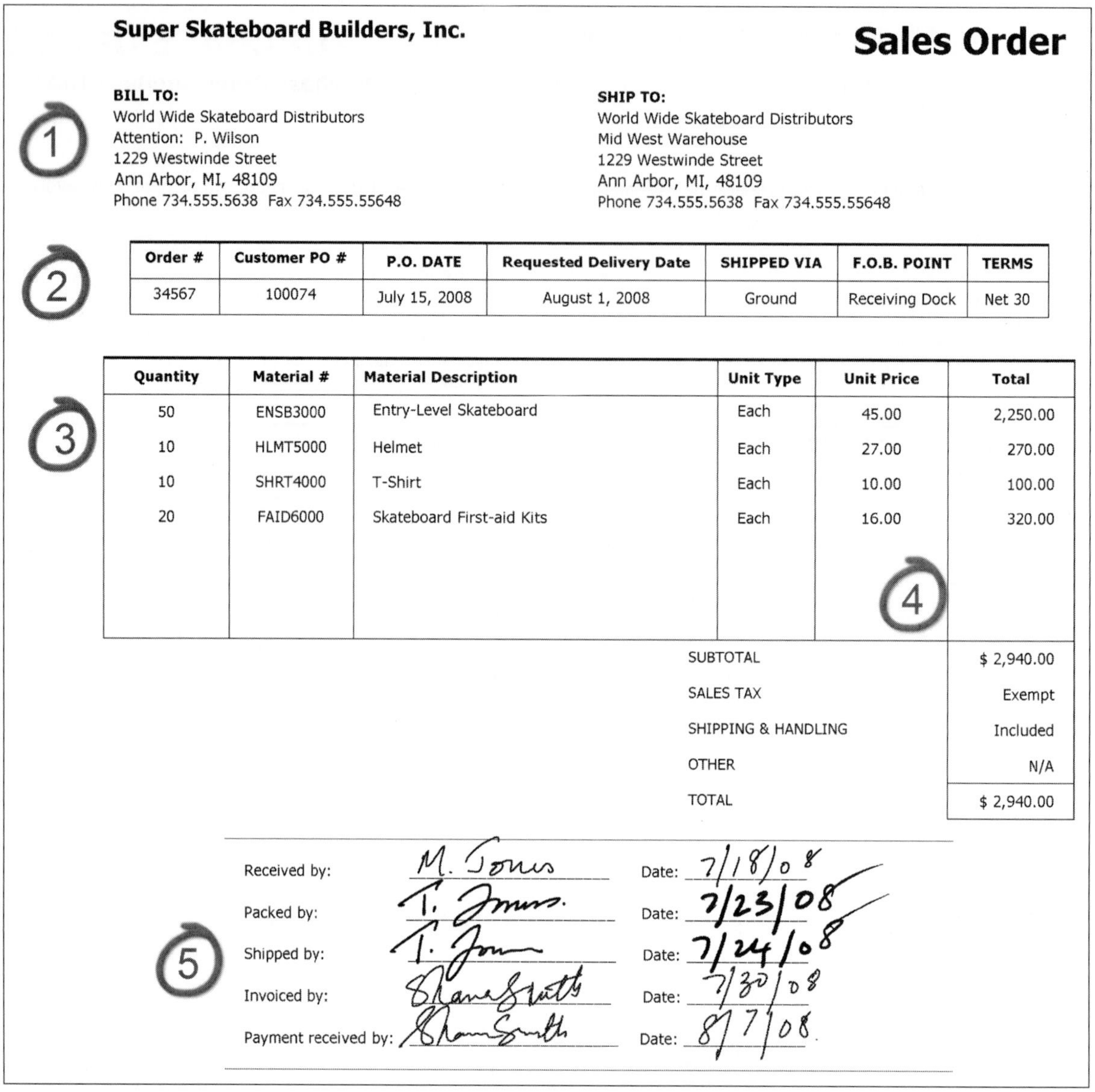

Super Skateboard Builders, Inc.

Sales Order

① BILL TO:
World Wide Skateboard Distributors
Attention: P. Wilson
1229 Westwinde Street
Ann Arbor, MI, 48109
Phone 734.555.5638 Fax 734.555.55648

SHIP TO:
World Wide Skateboard Distributors
Mid West Warehouse
1229 Westwinde Street
Ann Arbor, MI, 48109
Phone 734.555.5638 Fax 734.555.55648

②

Order #	Customer PO #	P.O. DATE	Requested Delivery Date	SHIPPED VIA	F.O.B. POINT	TERMS
34567	100074	July 15, 2008	August 1, 2008	Ground	Receiving Dock	Net 30

③

Quantity	Material #	Material Description	Unit Type	Unit Price	Total
50	ENSB3000	Entry-Level Skateboard	Each	45.00	2,250.00
10	HLMT5000	Helmet	Each	27.00	270.00
10	SHRT4000	T-Shirt	Each	10.00	100.00
20	FAID6000	Skateboard First-aid Kits	Each	16.00	320.00

④

SUBTOTAL	$ 2,940.00
SALES TAX	Exempt
SHIPPING & HANDLING	Included
OTHER	N/A
TOTAL	$ 2,940.00

⑤

Received by:	*M. Jones*	Date:	7/18/08
Packed by:	*T. Jmrs.*	Date:	7/23/08
Shipped by:	*T. Jom*	Date:	7/24/08
Invoiced by:	*Shane Smith*	Date:	7/30/08
Payment received by:	*Shane Smith*	Date:	8/7/08

Figure 4.5 Sales order

In our example in Figure 4.5, the sales order identifies the customer as World Wide Skateboard Distributors (area 1), with separate billing and shipping addresses. Separate addresses are typical because the materials will be shipped to a warehouse, which is not always located at the same address as the corporate offices where payment is handled. (Note, however, that for SSB the two addresses are the same.) SSB has assigned a unique order number (34567), but World Wide's PO number (100074) is also identified (area 2). The sales order also specifies the order and delivery dates and terms (area 2), the materials ordered (area 3), and the prices (area 4).

A second purpose of a sales order is to create an *internal record* of the customer's order that can be used to track progress. In addition to the data mentioned above, a sales order will include space to add data as the various steps in the fulfillment process are completed. These data will identify the individual(s) who completed each step, when, and where. In a manual environment, sales orders are multipart documents, and the data are filled in by hand. In contrast, an enterprise system automatically captures and stores these data. The data are then used to track the status of the order and to calculate the time required to complete various steps in fulfilling the order.

Once Matt creates the sales order, he will file a copy along with the customer PO. If the PO was preceded by an inquiry and quotation, he will file these documents with the sales order as well. He then sends the sales order to the warehouse for further processing.

Figure 4.5 shows the sales order in a completed state. That is, all the steps in the fulfillment process have been completed, the products have been shipped to the customer, and payment has been received. The bottom of the figure (area 5) shows that (1) Matt Jones received the customer PO on July 18 and prepared the sales order, (2) Tim in the warehouse packed and shipped the order on July 23 and 24, respectively, and (3) Shana sent the invoice on July 30 and recorded the payment from the customer on August 7. Thus, the entire process took about three weeks to complete.

Picking Document

When the warehouse receives the sales order, this is their indication to prepare the order for shipment. Preparing the shipment involves **picking** and **packing**. Picking is the act of retrieving the needed material from the warehouse. When the warehouse receives a sales order, it prepares a **picking document** (Figure 4.6). Some of the data in the picking document are the same as those contained in the sales order. In Figure 4.6, for example, the picking document includes the name and address of the customer (area 1) and the order number and the dates and terms of delivery (area 2). In addition, this document tells the picker how many of which items are part of this order and where these items are located in the warehouse, that is, the *storage locations*. In a small warehouse, a storage location can be something as simple as "finished goods area," whereas in larger warehouses it can include more specific information such as *aisle number*, *shelf number*, or *bin number*. In some cases, the storage location is not provided, and the picker adds it to the document once she or he has picked the material. In our example, the picking document indicates the material to be picked (area 3), quantities (area 4), and storage location 30 (area 5), which is the "finished goods" storage location in the SSB warehouse.

The items listed in a picking document are "picked" from the shelves in the specified locations and packed into the shipping box. The picker will note on the picking document the quantities of each item that were picked as well as the location they were picked from. In some cases the quantity picked is less than the quantity the customer ordered. In these cases only part of the order will be shipped and the remainder will be **backordered**, or sent on a later date when more products become available. It is also possible that the materials were picked from a storage location other than the one indicated on the picking document. This is the reason for confirming where they were picked from. In our example, the picking document indicates that Tim Jones (area 8) picked the exact quantities needed (area 6) from storage location 30 (area 7). In addition to completing the picking document, Tim will update the sales order to indicate that this step has been completed (area 5 in Figure 4.5).

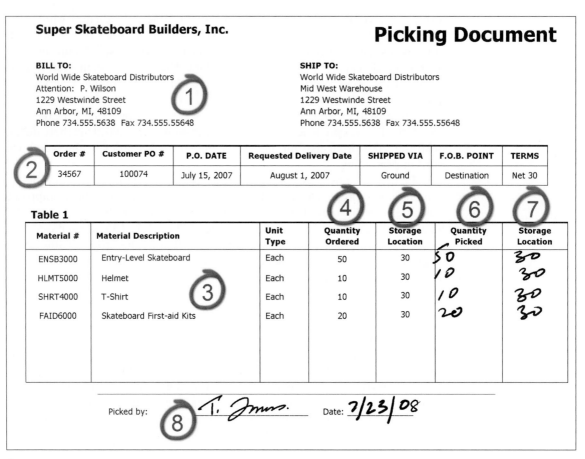

Figure 4.6 Picking document

Packing List

Packing is the act of preparing the material for shipment in a box or another suitable container. When the order is packed for shipment, another document, the **packing list** (Figure 4.7), is created. This document accompanies the shipment and specifies the items and quantities shipped. The customer then uses the packing list to verify that contents of the shipment match their original purchase order. Recall that we discussed packing lists in Chapter 3 from the perspective of the organization receiving the shipment. In this chapter, the perspective is that of the sending organization, but the data remain the same. In Figure 4.7, the packing list includes SSB's name and address (area 1), data about the order (area 2), packing and shipping information (3), customer billing and shipping addresses (area 4), and details about the material included in the shipment (area 5).

Once the shipment is sent, Tim will update the sales order, add the "shipped by" data (area 5 of Figure 4.5), and file a copy of the sales order with a copy of the packing slip and the picking document. He will then send the updated sales order to Shana in accounting to start the invoicing step.

Customer Invoice

Recall that in the procurement process the vendor sends an **invoice** to SSB. In contrast, in the fulfillment process SSB sends an invoice to the customer. The

Super Skateboard Builders, Inc   **Packing List**

1 Skateboard Drive
Grand Rapids, MI 49525
Phone (616) 555-1234
Fax (616) 555-1245

(1)

(2)

Order Date	Customer Contact	Customer Number	Customer PO #	Order Number	Shipped Via
July 15, 2007	P. Wilson	10054	1000074	34567	UPS Ground

Date Packed	Packed by	Checked by	Ship Date	Sales Rep	
July 23, 2007	TJ	TJ	July 24, 2007	Matt Jones	

(3)

(4)

Ship To:
World Wide Skateboard Distributors
Mid West Warehouse
1229 Westwinde Street
Ann Arbor, MI, 48109

Bill To:
World Wide Skateboard Distributors
Attention: P. Wilson
1229 Westwinde Street
Ann Arbor, MI, 48109

(5)

Material #	Description	Unit Weight (lb)	Unit Type	Order Quantity	Ship Quantity	Backorder Quantity	Weight (lb)
ENSB3000	Entry-Level Skateboard	7.50	Each	50	50	0	375.00
HLMT5000	Helmet	4.00	Each	10	10	0	40.00
SHRT4000	T-Shirt	0.75	Each	10	10	0	7.50
FAID6000	Skateboard First-aid Kits	2.00	Each	20	20	0	40.00

Total Shipment Weight 462.50

Comments: Backordered items will ship as they become available.

Please contact the Customer Service department at (616) 555-1234 with any questions or concerns.

Thank you for your order!

Figure 4.7 Packing list

invoice contains an itemized list of the materials sent or the services provided to the customer, along with the cost of the items plus discounts, taxes, shipping, and other charges, if applicable. The customer will match the information contained in the invoice with the information in the packing list from the shipment and their original purchase order to make sure that they received and are paying for what they ordered.

In our example, when Shana receives the sales order from Tim, she creates an invoice (Figure 4.8) for the material shipped and sends it to World Wide. The invoice includes customer addresses (area 1), basic information about the order (area 2), and details of the material prices and totals (area 3). Shana will update the sales order to indicate when the invoice was sent (area 5 of Figure 4.5) and then file it.

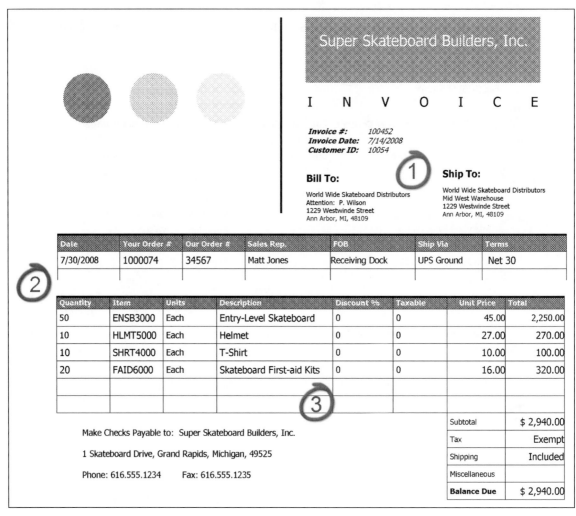

Figure 4.8 Customer invoice

Customer Payment

The final document relates to the **payment** made by the customer. In the simplest case, World Wide will send SSB a check for the amount indicated on the invoice. However, due to advances in technology, World Wide can now electronically transfer funds directly from its bank to SSB's bank. In this case, either World Wide or its bank will notify SSB of the transfer. When Shana receives payment, she will update the sales order to indicate this transaction (area 5 of Figure 4.5) and file it.

4.2.3 Information Flow

Recall from Chapter 3 that information flows occur at both the instance and process levels. In the fulfillment process, instance-level information indicates the status of a particular customer order. In contrast, process-level information assesses how well the process is being executed over time and helps the company identify and resolve any problems that are occurring.

Instance-Level Information

The ability to determine the status of a specific order is important to an organization for both its internal operations and its customer communications. As explained in Chapter 3, status information relates to the state of the order throughout a process, and much of the data needed to obtain this status are in the documents associated with the process. In the fulfillment process, for example, a company wants to know if the materials in the order have been shipped. If so, when, and were any materials backordered? If the shipment has been sent, has an invoice been sent? Has payment been received?

Consider our example of an order placed by Patrick Wilson from World Wide. If Patrick calls Matt to check the status of the order, how does Matt respond? He will retrieve the customer PO from his files. If there is no sales order with the PO, then Matt knows that he has not yet processed the PO. In this case he will inform Patrick of this and let him know when the PO will be processed. Of course, we're assuming that Matt is efficient with filing paperwork! In fact, the sales order could simply have been misfiled. What happens in this case?

Conversely, if Matt finds a sales order filed with the PO, then he knows that the order has been sent to the warehouse. Although this information clearly is valuable, someone must now call the warehouse to determine the status of the order. Does Matt tell the customer to make this call, or does he place the customer on hold and make the call himself? Going further, regardless of who actually calls, will the warehouse answer? They may be busy on the shop floor or at the storage areas. If someone does answer, say Tim, he now has to retrieve the sales order to determine if the order has been shipped, and, if so, when. If Tim finds the document, he can let Matt know if and when the material was shipped. Suppose, however, that Tim can't locate the sales order. What should he tell Matt? That the document has not yet reached the warehouse? That it is simply missing? That is has been misfiled? To further complicate matters, all this time the customer is waiting on the phone.

As you can see, obtaining simple status information in a manual environment can be time consuming and frustrating. Status information becomes increasingly important to customers when order volumes and values increase. Imagine a company that has placed hundreds of orders worth millions of dollars. It is easy to see how difficult it is to give such a customer accurate information regarding the status of its orders in a paper-based, manual environment.

Process-Level Information

Process-level information can be concerned either with steps in the process or with the process as a whole. Regarding individual steps, a company wants to identify orders that are open for more than a specified amount of time, and what is causing these orders to remain open. For example, if SSB has a target of shipping all orders within two days of receiving a customer PO, then John will want to identify those orders that have not been shipped for more than two days. To accomplish this task, he needs to assess at which step in the process the order is being held up. A company also wants to send invoices and receive payments as promptly as possible. Thus, if SSB has a target of sending invoices within 3 days of shipping and expects payment within 30 days, John will want to identify those orders that don't fit within these targets. He will then try to determine the causes and take corrective action.

Other process-level information is more aggregate in nature and is concerned with the process as a whole. For example, John is interested in the following questions:

1. What are SSB's best-selling products? Which products does it sell the least?
2. Who are SSB's best customers in terms of dollar sales and quantity? What do they purchase?
3. On average, how much time does SSB take to process a customer order?
4. What is the average value of a sales order?
5. What is the average time to complete each step in the process?
6. Which customers pay promptly? Which are habitually late?

The information needed to answer these questions must be compiled from the data that are generated during the many steps of the fulfillment process. In a manual environment, these data are stored in the various documents we have just discussed. To compile this information, employees must gather data from all the documents over a period of time and then organize, sort, and summarize these data and compute averages and other statistics. In a manual environment this is very time consuming, if not impossible.

4.2.4 Financial Impact

As we saw in the last chapter, some of the steps in a process have an impact on the financial position of the organization, whereas others do not. In this section we will determine which steps in the fulfillment process have an impact. Financial impact is recorded through changes in the accounts in the chart of account, based on the rules we discussed in Chapter 1. Table 4-1 summarizes the impact of the various steps in the fulfillment process. Figure 4.9 illustrates this impact.

TABLE 4-1   Financial Impact of Process Steps

Process Step	Income Statement Accounts Affected	Balance Sheet Accounts Affected
Receive Customer Inquiry	None	None
Create and Send Quotation	None	None
Receive Customer PO	None	None
Create Sales Order	None	None
Prepare Shipment	None	None
Send Shipment	Sales Revenue + Cost of Goods Sold +	Finished Goods Inventory − Accounts Receivable +
Prepare and Send Invoice	None	None
Receive Payment	None	Accounts Receivable − Cash (in the bank) +

Financial impact occurs when there is an exchange in value. Most of the steps in the process have no impact because they don't produce such an exchange. For example, when World Wide sends an inquiry to SSB, they are simply asking for information. Similarly, when SSB sends World Wide a quotation, they are simply

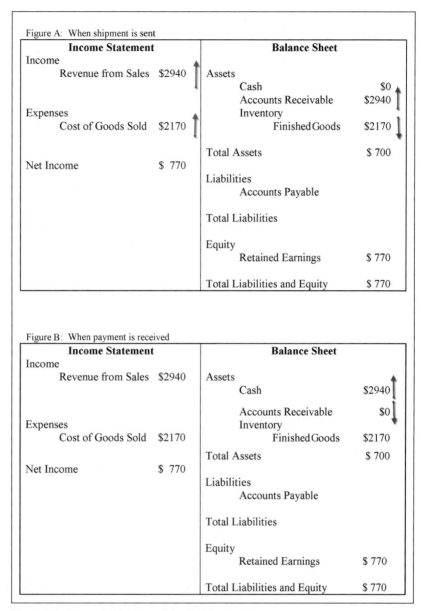

Figure 4.9 Financial impact of the fulfillment process

providing information. The receipt of a customer order is an agreement to buy something; no exchange of value occurs. An exchange of value takes place only when the order is shipped out and not before.

When the order is shipped out, there is an increase in sales revenue (income) and in accounts receivable (asset). In addition, there is a decrease in inventory (asset) and a corresponding increase in the cost of goods sold (expense). In Figure 4.9A, there is an increase in sales revenue and accounts receivable in the amount of $2,940 which is the total of the customer order. What about the value of inventory and the cost of goods sold? These totals are based on what SSB paid for these materials when it purchased them. The cost or value of all the materials in the order is $2,170. Thus, the value of finished goods inventory decreases, and the cost of goods sold increases by this amount. This exchange results in a net income of $770, which is transferred to retained earnings to balance out the balance sheet.

The next point in the process where a financial impact occurs is when payment is received from the customer. This exchange results in a decrease in accounts receivable (asset) and an increase in cash (asset). In Figure 4.9B, when SSB records a payment from World Wide, the accounts receivable decreases, and cash (in the bank) increases by $2,940.

▶ 4.3 ROLE OF ENTERPRISE SYSTEMS IN THE FULFILLMENT PROCESS

Recall from Chapter 3 that enterprise systems (ES) make business processes operate more effectively and efficiently by supporting the execution of the process, capturing and storing critical data, and monitoring performance. This section and Figure 4.10 explain how an ES contributes to the fulfillment process.

4.3.1 Execute the Process

As discussed earlier, the fulfillment process consists of a series of steps that must be completed in a particular sequence. The people involved in the process steps will log into the system and determine, for instance, which orders are ready for shipment and which ones are ready for billing. Because all the process data are stored in a common database, the system provides easy access to the data needed to complete the steps, such as what materials were ordered, when the shipment was sent, how

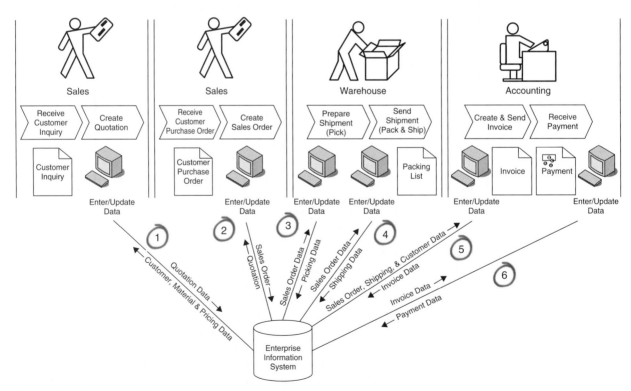

Figure 4.10   ES in the fulfillment process

much to charge, who to send the bill to, and the payment terms. Following is a description of how people use an enterprise system to complete each of the steps in the fulfillment process.

Create a Quotation

When SSB receives an inquiry from World Wide, Matt must create a quotation. He will log into the ERP system and access the program that creates quotations. He will then search for information about the customer (area 1 in Figure 4.10). If this information exists, the system will automatically retrieve the data that are relevant to the quotation, such as account number, address, and payment and delivery terms. Matt will compare these data to the information contained in the inquiry and will update the system, if necessary. He will then enter the products and quantities from the inquiry into the system. The system will retrieve information about the products, such as product number, description, and availability, and include this in the quotation. In addition, the system will retrieve product prices based either on specific agreements with the customer that exist in the system or on the standard price for the products. If any of the master data—material, customer, or pricing—are not in the system, then Matt must create them before he can proceed. (If you have questions concerning master data and other types of data in an enterprise system, please review the discussion in Chapter 2.)

The system will automatically calculate taxes, shipping charges, and totals. It will also include the current date and note that Matt is creating the quotation. Matt is able to review the data in the quotation and make adjustments as needed. Once he is satisfied, he will save the quotation in the system (area 1 in Figure 4.10). At this time, the system will automatically generate and add a unique quotation number. Matt now has the option to print the quotation and send it to the customer by fax or mail or to have the system e-mail the quotation directly. All the data associated with the quotation are now stored in the common database in the enterprise system and are easily accessible to support subsequent steps in the process.

Create a Sales Order

When Matt receives World Wide's PO, he will log into the system and search for a previously created quotation. If one exists, he will retrieve it (area 2 in Figure 4.10) to see if it matches the PO. If it does, he will use the data in the quotation to create a new sales order, making any necessary changes. For instance, the customer may have inquired about 100 skateboards but decided to order 200.

If no quotation exists, Matt will have to manually enter all the data that would have been in a quotation to create the sales order. Additional data such as the delivery date and which location the order should be shipped from are suggested by the system automatically based on business rules, such as the earliest possible delivery date or the nearest warehouse. Matt can either accept these suggestions or override them based on customer requests or for other reasons. Once Matt is satisfied with the data in the sales order, he will save it (area 2 in Figure 4.10). At this point the system will generate a unique sales order number and note that Matt is the person who created the order.

All the data associated with the sales order are now stored in the common database. Persons in the warehouse can log into the system periodically to see if there are any sales orders that require their attention. Alternatively, the system can be configured to automatically notify persons in the Warehouse, via e-mail, that shipments are ready to be picked and packed.

Prepare Shipment

When Tim logs into the system from the warehouse, the system will retrieve the **delivery due list**, that is, a list of sales orders that must be prepared for shipment today to meet the required delivery dates. The system will determine which orders are due for delivery based on the required delivery dates and estimates of the time needed to prepare and ship the order. These estimates are part of the master data in the system, and they are periodically adjusted to reflect the actual times needed to complete tasks. The sales order for World Wide (Figure 4.5) specifies a desired delivery date of August 1. If the average time to prepare the shipment is one day and the estimated shipment time is three days, the system will make the order due for delivery no later than four working days prior to August 1, which is July 28.

Figure 4.11 is an example of a delivery due list from an enterprise system. It lists three orders (#42, 43, and 44 in area 1) that are due for delivery as of some specified date. It also identifies the different materials in the orders (area 4), the *confirmed quantity*, or quantity the customer ordered (area 2), and the *open quantity*, which is the quantity that needs to be delivered (area 3). Note that the confirmed and open quantities are identical. However, these values would be different if a partial shipment had previously been sent.

When an order is selected, the system will retrieve the relevant data from the sales order, material master, and other sources (area 3 in Figure 4.10). It will then use these data to create the documents needed for picking and packing the order—the picking document and packing list. Tim will take the picking document (in printed form or on a handheld computing device), go to the specified location, pick the items from the shelves, and pack them in a shipping box. He also will verify that the contents in the box match the packing list, and he will include the packing list with the shipment. He will then take the shipping box to the **shipping**

Activities Due for Shipping "Sales orders, fast display"

Light	Client	SD Doc.	OriginDoc.	Item	Item	ConfirmQty	Open qty	Unit	Dlv.qty	Material	Cum.qty	SU
∞	610		43	40		20	20	EA	0	FAID6000	20	EA
∞	610		43	30		15	15	EA	0	SHRT4000	15	EA
∞	610		43	20		15	15	EA	0	HLMT5000	15	EA
∞	610		43	10		30	30	EA	0	ENSB3000	30	EA
∞	610		42	40		20	20	EA	0	FAID6000	20	EA
∞	610		42	30		10	10	EA	0	SHRT4000	10	EA
∞	610		42	20		10	10	EA	0	HLMT5000	10	EA
∞	610		42	10		50	50	EA	0	ENSB3000	50	EA
∞	610		44	10		200	200	EA	0	ENSB3000	200	EA
∞	610		44	20		70	70	EA	0	HLMT5000	70	EA
∞	610		44	30		120	120	EA	0	SHRT4000	120	EA
∞	610		44	40		100	100	EA	0	FAID6000	100	EA

Figure 4.11 Delivery due list
Source: Copyright SAP AG 2008

point or the location in the warehouse where the shipment is picked up or loaded onto a truck. He will then return to his workstation, log into the system, retrieve the picking document, and enter the quantity picked and the storage location. The system will automatically include the date and note that Tim is completing this step in the process.

Send Shipment

When the packaged order is picked up by the shipper (for example, FedEx, DHL, UPS), Tim will retrieve the order from the system and indicate that the shipment has been sent (area 4 in Figure 4.10). This step triggers a variety of accounting entries, such as those discussed in the section on financial impact. Once again the relevant data, such as the date, the person completing the task, and information related to the shipper, are captured and stored in the common database.

Create and Send Invoice

As soon as the order has been shipped, it is ready for invoicing. The system can be configured to handle this step in a number of ways: (1) It can automatically generate an invoice and e-mail it to World Wide, (2) it can send Shana an e-mail alert to send an invoice, or (3) it can simply wait until Shana logs into the system and requests a **billing due list**, which, as its name implies, is a list of orders for which billing is due.

Figure 4.12 is an example of a billing due list in an enterprise system. It shows that billing is due for three shipments. Among other things, the list identifies the customer (area 1) and the document number of the delivery document, which will show the details of the order (area 2).

When Shana logs in and retrieves the billing due list, she will select one of the items on the list for processing. The system will retrieve and display all the relevant data (area 5 in Figure 4.10). When Shana is satisfied with the accuracy of the data, she will save the invoice in the system (area 5 in Figure 4.10) and then send the invoice to the customer by mail, fax or e-mail.

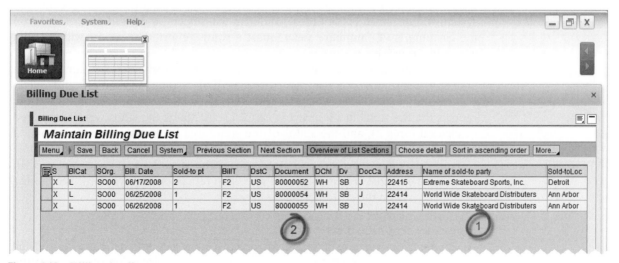

Figure 4.12 Billing due list
Source: Copyright SAP AG 2008

Receive and Process Payment

The final step in the process is to record a payment from the customer. When World Wide sends a payment (a check or a notification of electronic funds transfer), Shana will log into the system and retrieve their account (area 6 in Figure 4.10). The system will display all their invoices. Shana will then select the invoices against which the payment is to be applied and save the data (area 6 in Figure 4.10). The system will then mark the invoice as paid and will update the relevant accounts (bank and receivables), as discussed in the section on financial impact.

4.3.2 Capture and Store Process Data

The next role of an enterprise system is to capture and store all the data that are generated from the various process steps. This role is evident from the discussion in the previous section. During each step we described, the system obtains data from various sources, consolidates them, and stores them for later use. Sources of data include master data already in the system (e.g., customer, material, and pricing), data created in a previous process step, user-entered data, and system-generated data (e.g., dates and identities of persons completing the step). In some cases, the data are used in later steps in the process. In other cases the data are used to generate information that the company will use to monitor the process.

4.3.3 Monitor the Process

Instance-level Information

The ES helps us monitor the state of the process at both the instance and process levels. At the instance level, a company might wish to determine where in the process a particular customer order is. To do this it provides the system with relevant information, such as an order number. In turn, the system retrieves the data associated with the order and displays a status report. This report will indicate which step in the process the order is currently in.

To illustrate this process more clearly, let's refer back to World Wide's purchase from SSB. If Patrick Wilson calls SSB to check the status of the order, Matt will log into the system and search for all sales orders associated with World Wide. The system will display a list of orders, and Tim will select the desired order (based on the customer's PO number) and request a status report. The report will tell Tim where in the process the order is.

Recall that in the manual process, obtaining this information was cumbersome and time consuming. In contrast, with an ERP system, it is simple and quick. Figures 4.13 and 4.14 provide examples of status reports for two orders. These reports list the steps in the process (area 1), the dates the steps were completed or cleared (area 2), and the status of the step (area 3). If a step is not completed (or cleared), then the date is the status as of the indicated date. The first example (Figure 4.13) shows an order in which all of the steps have been completed. In the second example (Figure 4.14) the only step remaining is payment ("accounting document") from the customer.

Process-level Information

A company can retrieve a variety of reports to view both the status of specific steps in the process and the process as a whole. In our discussion of executing the process, we already have discussed reports that focus on specific steps, such as the

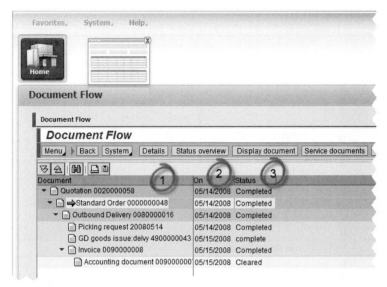

Figure 4.13 Order status report—completed order
Source: Copyright SAP AG 2008

delivery due list and billing due list. Figure 4.15 is an example of a report that provides data concerning the process as a whole. Specifically, it includes a summary of customer orders for the months of January, February, and March (area 1) and information regarding delays for orders in January (area 2). The reasons for delays are summarized in the accompanying pie chart (area 3).

The summary for (area 1) shows that SSB had 7, 11, and 15 orders for the three months. February was the best month in terms of orders shipped on time (within two days of receiving the customer PO). January and March were not very good months. In fact, more than half the orders in January were late. When this report

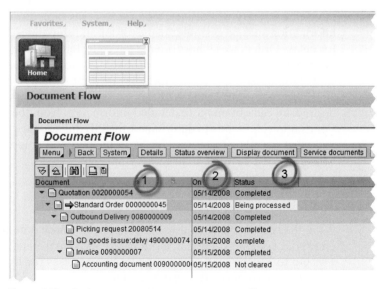

Figure 4.14 Order status report—payment pending
Source: Copyright SAP AG 2008

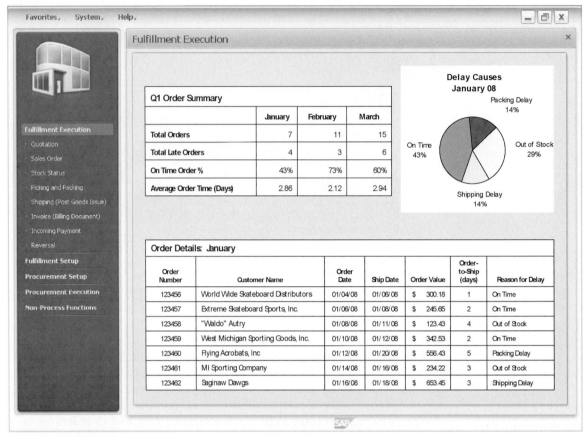

Figure 4.15   Fulfillment analytics
Source: Copyright SAP AG 2008

is displayed on the screen, John can "drill down" for more details. Clicking on the month of January will display the order details table (area 2). This table provides information such as customer name, order and ship dates, order value, and reasons for delay. Orders were most often delayed in January due to **stock out**, that is, SSB did not have sufficient products in inventory to meet customer demand. The pie chart summarizes the reasons for delay for January.

Once John understands the reasons for the process not working as well as desired, he can obtain more detailed information from the system about the causes. For example, he wants to determine why SSB did not have enough stock of products and what exactly caused the delays in picking and shipping. He will then decide what corrective actions to take.

▶ 4.4 EXERCISE USING SIMULATED SAP ERP

As in the case of the procurement chapter, it is now time for you to experience an enterprise system in action in a simulated SAP environment.

Go to WileyPLUS and complete the exercises for this chapter. The exercises consist of three parts, two exercises and a short quiz. The first exercise will guide you through the steps in the fulfillment process, whereas in the second one you will complete the steps on your own, without any guidance.

The exercises will take you through the following steps that have been discussed in this chapter:

1. Receive customer inquiry
2. Create a quotation
3. Receive a customer purchase order
4. Create a sales order
5. Prepare the shipment (pick and pack)
6. Send the shipment (post goods issue)
7. Create a customer invoice
8. Receive a customer payment

In the final part, a short quiz will test your knowledge of the fulfillment process. Here you will complete a series of multiple-choice questions related to key concepts in the chapter and exercises. Your instructor will direct you to the location of the quiz. After you have completed the quiz, the system will grade it and send your score to your professor's grade book. You may view your score in the gradebook tab of WileyPLUS.

As before, please pay attention to what you are doing and understand why the actions are necessary to execute the process. You may repeat these exercises as often as needed to thoroughly understand the fulfillment process and how an enterprise system supports it.

► CHAPTER SUMMARY

In this chapter we have described a very simple fulfillment process, consisting of a few simple steps. In reality, fulfillment processes are far more complex. However, our purpose is to help you understand the fundamentals of fulfillment in terms of the four flows—physical, data, document, and information. In addition, the chapter illustrates the critical role of enterprise systems in executing the fulfillment process and providing meaningful information about the process.

A manual fulfillment process includes several steps that must be completed in a particular sequence in different parts of the organization—sales, warehouse, and accounting. When the sales department receives a customer inquiry, it sends a quotation to the customer. The customer considers the quotation and submits a purchase order (PO), which is a binding agreement to purchase the stated materials. In response to a customer PO, a sales order is created. A sales order standardizes the data needed to fill the order and is a means to communicate with other people involved in the process. Each person in the process completes his or her step, adds the relevant data, and forwards the sales order to the next person. In the warehouse, two additional documents—the picking document and the packing list—are needed to prepare and send the shipment. Once the order is shipped, someone

in the accounting department creates an invoice. The final step is to receive and record payment from the customer.

Organizations want information about the process at both the instance and process levels. This information is necessary to determine the state of a particular order and to monitor the process as a whole to detect, avoid, or solve problems. In a manual environment, it is very difficult to obtain this information because the needed data are scattered across numerous documents in different parts of the organization.

An enterprise system makes the fulfillment process more efficient and effective. It keeps all the data associated with the process in one central database that is accessible to all the persons involved in the execution of the process. The system also facilitates communication between the persons involved in the process. Finally, an enterprise system can automate some of the steps in the process. Because all the data about the process are located in a common database, obtaining information about one order or the process as a whole is very easy. In turn, the availability of information when it is needed makes it easy to monitor the process and to detect, avoid, and correct problems.

In today's hypercompetitive global marketplace, companies cannot compete effectively if they must execute their fulfillment process manually. Customers today expect instant visibility into the status of their orders and next-day shipments, and companies must optimize their fulfillment process to meet these expectations. Enterprise systems make this possible by improving communication and coordination between and among functional areas. Better coordination leads to increased efficiency as tasks are completed faster and with fewer errors. This is particularly true in highly automated environments where the ES can automatically manage and complete many of these tasks. The result is reduced lead times and cycle times, increased visibility, reduced inventory, and ultimately better customer service and competitiveness.

▶ KEY TERMS

backorder	delivery due list	picking	shipping point
billing due list	invoice	picking document	stock out
configure-to-order	packing	quotation	
customer inquiry	packing list	sales order	
customer purchase order	payment	sell-from-stock	

▶ REVIEW QUESTIONS

1. Explain the difference between sell-from-stock and configure-to-order strategies

2. Explain the key steps in a basic fulfillment process.

3. Briefly describe the key documents in the fulfillment process in terms of their role in the process.

4. Explain the difference between a backorder and a stock out.

5. Define the following terms:
   (a) Mode of shipment
   (b) Storage location
   (c) Open quantity
   (d) Delivered quantity

▶ ASSIGNMENTS

1. The fulfillment process described in this chapter is deliberately very simple. Based on your experiences or by talking to someone in a local company, define and describe a more complex fulfillment process in terms of the physical, document, and data flows. What functions of the organizations will be involved in this process?

2. This chapter provides some examples of instance-level and process-level information. Identify two more examples of each type of information and explain what data will be needed to generate this information. What is the source of these data?

3. Identify some of the key problems associated with the manual, or paper-based, fulfillment process. How does an enterprise system eliminate or reduce the impact of these problems.

4. SSB receives a purchase order for the following materials from World Wide Skateboard Distributors. Create all the documents necessary to document the process used to fill this order. You can search the Internet for examples of the documents included in this chapter or you can create them using a word processor.

- 60 Entry-level skateboards

- 30 T-shirts

- 10 First aid kits

5. For the process in question 3, explain the financial impact of the process steps on SSB. Draw a diagram similar to the figure used in this chapter to explain the financial impact.

CHAPTER **5**

The Production Process

Learning Objectives

After completing this chapter you will be able to:

▶ Describe the steps in the production process.

▶ Explain the role of different functional areas in efficiently and effectively completing the process.

▶ Identify the key data, document, and information flows associated with the production process.

▶ Explain the role of enterprise systems in supporting the process.

Historically, SSB has dealt exclusively with trading goods, which it purchases from its vendors and then immediately resells to its customers. Now, rather than simply reselling other companies' skateboards, John wants SSB to beginning producing its own. This clearly is a big step, and John is wondering exactly what it will involve. He recognizes that SSB will now have to purchase the raw materials, or parts, it needs to make the skateboards. However, he has many questions: What parts will SSB need, and in what quantities? After SSB purchases the parts, how does it assemble them to make the skateboards? Finally, how should he keep track of all this work? John vaguely remembers something about bills of material, routing, and accounting from his classes. Now he wishes that he had paid more attention.

In this chapter, we will discuss the production process, also known as the *plan-to-produce* process. The production process includes all the steps necessary to make the finished goods from components. We will begin by illustrating a simple production process in terms of the data, document, and information flows. We will conclude by examining the role of enterprise systems in supporting the production process. Whereas in the chapters on the procurement and fulfillment process we explained the impact of the processes on the company's financial position, we will omit this discussion in this chapter. Even a simplified discussion of the financial impact of the production processes requires an understanding of accounting concepts related to allocating labor and overhead costs, and this is beyond the scope of this book.

▶ 5.1 KEY CONCEPTS AND ASSUMPTIONS

The production process is more complex than the procurement and fulfillment processes. Therefore, it is essential that we begin this chapter by defining certain key concepts and assumptions. Specifically, we focus on different types of production processes and strategies as well as master data regarding bills of material, work centers, and product routings.

5.1.1 Production Processes and Strategies

There are many different types of production processes, and they can be classified in different ways. For example, production can involve either **assembling** or **manufacturing**. Assembling involves taking a number of component materials, such as a board, nuts, and bolts, and putting them together to produce the desired finished product, such as a skateboard. In contrast, manufacturing involves taking raw materials, such as plastic pellets, and creating something from them, such as a plate or a cup. Another way to classify production is in terms of **discrete manufacturing** (e.g., furniture, computers, plates, cups) versus **process manufacturing** (e.g., oil and gas). A detailed discussion of these concepts is beyond the scope of this book. Skateboard production at SSB is a discrete process that consists of assembling the skateboard from component materials.

Some companies produce goods only in response to direct customer orders, whereas others create an inventory of products that they can store and then use later to meet customer demands. The former strategy is called **make-to-order**, and the latter is referred to as **make-to-stock**. A comparison between Apple Computers and Dell Corporation illustrates these two strategies (see Business Processes in Practice 5-1). SSB uses the make-to-stock strategy, meaning that it maintains an inventory of skateboards and then uses that inventory to fill customer orders.

▶ *BUSINESS PROCESSES IN PRACTICE 5-1*

APPLE INC. VERSUS DELL

Computers clearly have become an essential feature of modern life. Given this fact, if you managed a computer manufacturer, which production strategy would you select: make-to-stock or make-to-order? In fact, the computer industry utilizes both strategies. Let's take a closer look.

A good example of a company that uses the make-to-stock strategy is Apple Inc. Although Apple uses the configure-to-order process for Mac orders from its online store as discussed in Business Processes in Practice 4-1 from Chapter 4, it uses the make-to-stock process for Macs sold in its Apple stores. Apple first estimates the consumer demand for its Mac computers. It then calculates its available manufacturing capacity and the quantities of raw material it will need to build enough computers to meet this demand. Apple's strategy is to purchase raw materials and reserve manufacturing capacity ahead of time to maximize the cost efficiencies of buying materials in bulk quantities and doing large production runs. Apple then produces a specific quantity of each Mac model and ships them from the factory to the Apple stores and other retail outlets for sale. When customers come into an Apple store, they expect that the computer they want to buy will be there and that they can take it home immediately.

Because Apple uses a make-to-stock strategy, the company must pay extremely close attention to both its retail sales and the amount of finished goods inventory it has in stock to estimate its demand as accurately as possible. If Apple overestimates the demand for a particular product, the company will be stuck with a large inventory of very expensive finished goods that customers don't want to buy and will decrease in value while they sit on the shelf. Conversely, if it underestimates the demand for a product, customers who want to purchase the computer will be told it is "out of stock." They will then have two options: Either place a "back order" and wait until the store gets resupplied with inventory, or shop for the product at a different store. Either outcome will make consumers very unhappy and could result in lost sales.

In contrast, one of Apple's major competitors—Dell—employs a make-to-order production strategy. Dell was the first company in the industry to build computers only after they had received a firm order and thus knew exactly what product the customer wanted. Because Dell does not have retail outlets like Apple (although recently it has tested some retail partnerships), the company relies primarily on telephone and Internet sales channels for the majority of their sales. In contrast to Apple customers, then, when Dell customers place an order, they anticipate that they will have to wait a few days for the computer to be produced and delivered.

After the customer places an order, Dell typically assembles the computer from raw materials it has on hand and then ships it directly to the customer. Unlike Apple, then, Dell does not need to be very concerned with estimating demand for its finished products because it knows exactly what customers want based on the orders they are placing. However, Dell must be extremely careful in purchasing raw materials and managing its production capacity. Because its production runs are very small—sometimes one at a time—it must estimate its raw material needs and production scheduling based on an unknown customer demand. Dell is especially susceptible to oversupply or undersupply of raw materials and production capacity shortages or idleness if it mismanages its production planning process. If Dell does not have enough raw materials on hand or enough production capacity, customers will have to wait much longer for their computers to be shipped. Conversely, if the company has too much raw material or production capacity, it loses money.

Although Dell's customers are accustomed to waiting a few days for their computers to arrive, they might not be pleased if their deliveries are delayed for several weeks due to a shortage of raw materials or a backlog of production orders. Alternatively, Dell's profitability will suffer if its production lines are idle or its warehouses are filled with unused raw materials.

Both Apple and Dell have chosen a production strategy that maximizes their profitability. Apple believes that by controlling the entire buying experience through their Internet and physical stores, they can attract more customers. This strategic objective drives Apple to place a much higher emphasis on having products available in the store when a customer comes there to shop, which increases the likelihood that she or he will make a purchase. Apple gets significant cost savings through large, planned production runs and close coordination with retail sales data coming from their online and physical stores. Thus, the make-to-stock production process is probably the best strategy for Apple and its customers.

In the case of Dell, the make-to-order production process fits well with the company's rapid assembly and standardized products. Dell's customers are comfortable ordering a computer that they have never seen because they know that Dell uses high-quality, industry-standard components. They have also learned to trust that Dell can ship them a finished computer in just a few days, and they are comfortable waiting for it to arrive rather than picking it up in a store.

In essence, the preferences and behavior of each company's customers determine, to a great extent, the production process for each company. Apple's customers want to touch and experience the product in a retail store, whereas Dell's customers are happy to buy something over the phone or the Internet. Each company has optimized its production process to its specific set of customer requirements and its own internal profitability goals and cost structure.

Source: Compiled from Apple company reports; "Back to the Future at Apple," *Business Week*, May 25, 1998; "The Build-to-Order Dilemma," *MacWorld*, May 1, 1998; Dell company reports; and "Supply Meets Demand at Dell Inc.," *Accenture*, accessed July 22, 2008, http://www.accenture.com/Global/Services/By_Industry/Communications/Access_Newsletter/Article_Index/SupplyComputer.htm.

5.1.2 Master Data in the Production Process

Recall that in the procurement and fulfillment processes, the materials procured and sold were trading goods, that is, materials that are simply purchased and then resold. Therefore, the master data focus largely on customers, vendors, and materials. In contrast, the production process involves a different type of material, namely, an assembled material, or product. In other words, material is produced by assembling (putting together) several component materials. For this reason, the production process involves three additional types of master data: bill of material, work center, and product routing. Let's take a closer look at each one.

Bill of Material

A **bill of materials** (BOM) identifies all the materials or parts needed to make one unit of a finished product. It is based on the design of the product. **Product**

design is a separate process in organizations that is concerned with creating new products based on such factors as market research and new production techniques. The result of the product design process is an **engineering drawing** of the product. Figure 5.1 illustrates an engineering drawing for the standard skateboard that SSB is going to produce. It is a visual representation of the product and its components. A bill of materials is derived from the engineering drawing. Figure 5.2 illustrates the component materials needed to create one standard skateboard.

The standard skateboard is made up of eight components parts, which we list below. The numbers in parentheses indicate the quantity of each component that is needed to make one skateboard.

- Lock nut (8)
- Bolt (8)
- Packing box (1)
- SSB label (1)
- Grip tape (1)
- Riser pads (2)
- Standard deck (1)
- Standard truck assembly (2)

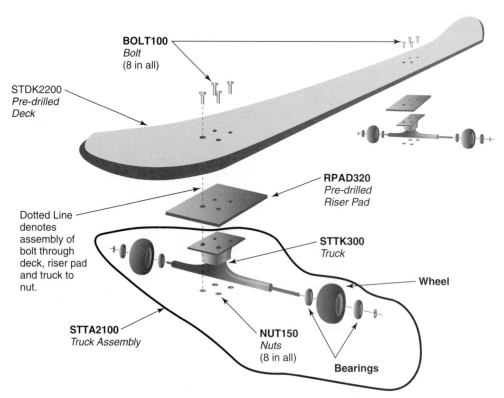

STSB2000 Standard Skateboard

BOLT100
Bolt
(8 in all)

STDK2200
Pre-drilled
Deck

RPAD320
Pre-drilled
Riser Pad

Dotted Line
denotes
assembly of
bolt through
deck, riser pad
and truck to
nut.

STTK300
Truck

Wheel

STTA2100
Truck Assembly

NUT150
Nuts
(8 in all)

Bearings

Figure 5.1 Engineering drawing of the standard skateboard

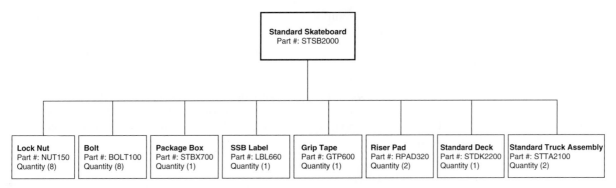

Figure 5.2 Bill of materials for the standard skateboard

Work Centers

The actual task of creating the product is accomplished in **work centers**. One or more tasks or operations can be completed in a work center. Figure 5.3 shows the plant layout for SSB, Inc. Note the three work centers in the upper left section of the figure.

- 200: Material Staging Area. In this work center all the components needed to create the products are obtained and readied for use in subsequent work centers.

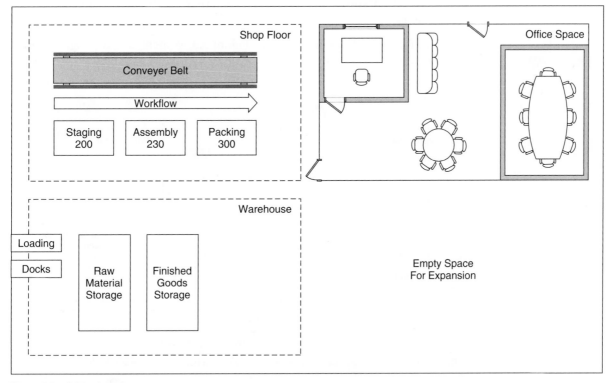

Figure 5.3 SSB plant layout

- 230: Final Assembly Area. Here the various components are assembled into the standard skateboard.
- 300: Packaging and Inspection Area. Finally, the skateboard is inspected and packed.

The needed material are moved from the raw material storage area onto the shop floor. There it is transported between the work centers using the conveyer belt. Once the skateboards are produced, they are moved into the finished goods storage area.

Product Routing

Product routings define the steps or operations necessary to create the product. For each operation, the routing lists the work center where the operation is to be conducted, the time allocated for each operation, and the material to be used in each operation. Figure 5.4 shows the routing for the standard skateboard produced at SSB. The routing consists of the following six operations:

1. **Material staging.** The component materials needed to make the skateboard are *staged*; that is, they are obtained and readied.

2. **Skateboard assembly.** The materials are assembled into a skateboard.

3. **Initial inspection.** To ensure that assembly step was completed properly.

4. **Packing.** The skateboard is packed in a packing box.

5. **Final inspection.** A final inspection is performed prior to placing the skateboard in inventory.

6. **Move to storage.** The finished materials (skateboards) are placed into storage.

If you look back for a minute to Figure 5.3, you can see the logical flow of materials along the steps and activities involved in producing a standard skateboard.

	Staging **Work Center 200**			*Assembly* **Work Center 230**	*Packing* **Work Center 300**

10	200	5*		Stage Material	Bolts, Nuts, Label, Griptape, Riser Pad, Standard Deck, Standard Truck Assembly
20	230	6		Assemble Skateboard	Bolts, Nuts, Label, Griptape, Riser Pad, Standard Deck, Standard Truck Assembly
30	300	1		Initial Inspection	
40	300	1		Pack in packaging box	Standard Packaging Box
50	300	1		Final Inspection	
60	300	5*		Move to Storage	

*Note: The time needed to stage material and move to storage is for batches of 50 skateboards
All other times are per skateboard.

Figure 5.4 Product routing for standard skateboard

Materials move in a clockwise direction from the warehouse through the work centers and then back to the warehouse.

The master data in SSB's production process are very simple. We have selected this example so that we can focus on the processes and not get lost in the data. The Boeing Corporation case illustrated in, Business Processes in Practice 5-2 describes a much more complex production process.

▶ *BUSINESS PROCESSES IN PRACTICE 5-2*

A COMPLEX PRODUCTION PROCESS AT BOEING CORPORATION

The production process used by SSB in this book has been extremely simplified to illustrate the core concepts of the process. SSB has a very small facility that is operated by a handful of employees and produces only one simple product. By contrast, most manufacturing companies in the "real world" operate much more complex and intricate production processes.

For example, Boeing—the world's largest manufacturer of commercial and military aircraft—operates the largest manufacturing facility in the world. The main production facility at Boeing's Everett, Washington, plant is the largest building in the world, covering nearly 100 acres (40 hectares) of space. More than 25,000 employees work in the facility, split over three shifts, and produce the Boeing 747, 767, 777, and 787 airplanes on several production lines. Operating at maximum capacity, the plant can manufacture up to seven 747s and 777s per month and up to five 767s per month.

Bill of Materials

The bill of materials for the Boeing 747 includes more than 6 million parts, and the BOMs for the 767 and 777 contain more than 3 million parts each. To make things even more complex, all those parts are subject to intensive quality and reliability checks, and they are inspected multiple times before, during, and after they are installed.

Work Centers

The work centers at the Boeing facility aren't "fixed" like the ones at SSB. The Boeing work centers actually move along the production line on wheels or tracks because the production line is constantly in motion. Cranes and rail cars deliver raw materials and sub-assemblies to each work center.

Product Routing

Because airplanes are produced on a moving assembly line, raw materials are delivered to different points along the line as needed. It would be impossible to stage all the materials for each plane at the beginning of the line. As the production line moves, the developing airplane proceeds toward the enormous doors at the end of the building, which connect to the runway at the airport.

Given the complexity of the BOM, product routing, and assembly process, the Boeing plant has one of the most robust and reliable ES environments on earth. Boeing must order, track, and distribute millions of parts to the right place at the right time—every time. They must also do all of this in the world's largest and busiest factory.

Boeing 747 Moving Production Line
Source: © Louie Psihoyos/Science Faction/Getty Images.

5.1.3 A Basic Production Process

Now that we understand the key concepts related to production, we shift our focus to the business processes associated with production. We emphasize the word *business* to distinguish this process from the operations or steps involved in physically creating the skateboard. We examined these operations in the section on routings. Here we are interested in the larger process the organization implements to produce the needed products.

Before we proceed, however, we need to consider once again a key point, namely, that production processes in organizations are very complex. To explain them in plain terms and to focus on the key steps in these processes, we must make some simplifying assumptions. These assumptions are related to the availability of raw material in the warehouse, the **production capacity** in the work centers to produce the necessary skateboards, and the quality of the production process. Specifically, we will assume that the necessary raw materials are always available and they are of high quality. After all, SSB does have an excellent procurement process, as we saw in Chapter 3.

Production capacity is the number of skateboards the shop floor can produce in a specified amount of time, such as per hour or per day. This is determined by how much time it takes to make each skateboard. The product routing (Figure 5.4) indicates that it takes 9 minutes to make one skateboard (operations 20 to 50). In addition, it takes 5 minutes to stage enough material for up to 50 skateboards and another 5 minutes to move up to 50 skateboards into storage.

The time taken to make 50 skateboards is calculated to be 460 minutes in Table 5-1. This is approximately 8 hours. Thus the production capacity is 50 skateboards per day. We will assume that production orders at SSB are authorized in batches of 50 or multiples of 50.

TABLE 5-1 Production Time Calculation

Operation Number	Operation Name	Time needed for 50 SB (minutes)
10	Stage Material	5
20	Assemble SB	300
30	Inspect Deck	50
40	Pack in Packing Box	50
50	Final Inspection	50
60	Move to Storage	5
	Total Time	$460 = 7.66$ hours

Finally, we will assume that (1) the production process always works smoothly, (2) all the skateboards pass the final inspection, and (3) there is no need for rework. Obviously, in the real world of production these assumptions are not always realistic. We use them strictly as academic devices to make the discussion of production more manageable.

5.1.4 Physical Flow

Figure 5.5 highlights the various functional areas that are involved in making skateboards and the necessary steps that are performed in each area. In the make-to-stock strategy used by SSB, the event that triggers the production process is the need to increase product inventory. Many sophisticated techniques exist for

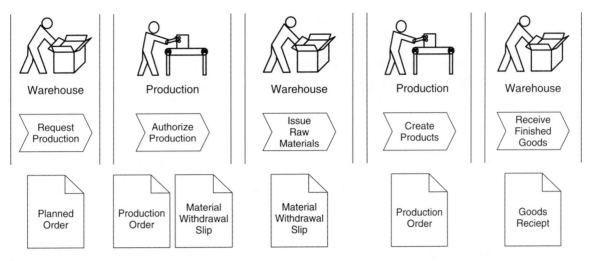

Figure 5.5   A basic production process

determining optimal inventory levels. However, SSB, Inc. employs a very simple technique. When the number of skateboards in inventory has been reduced to a predetermined quantity, David Bloomberg, the warehouse manager responsible for maintaining adequate inventory, requests that more skateboards be produced. This *request for production* is sent to the plant manager, Catherine VanderBos, who *authorizes the production*. The workers in the shop floor, Charlie Skivers and Mark McKendry, obtain the necessary materials from Tim Jones in the warehouse (*issue raw material*). These materials are then used in the shop floor to assemble the required quantity of skateboards (*create products*). Finally, the assembled products are placed in storage in the warehouse (*receive finished goods*)

As with procurement and fulfillment, it is necessary to understand how the various people involved in the production process know that they need to complete their part in the process. How does the shop floor know when to make skateboards? How does the person in the warehouse know what material and quantities to issue to the shop floor? Much of the communication among the various people involved in the process is accomplished using documents. In the next section we discuss the documents associated with the steps in the production process as well as the key data contained in these documents. This is similar to the approach we took in the chapters related to procurement and fulfillment.

5.1.5 Document and Data Flow

Planned Order
The production process begins with a request for production in the form of a **planned order** (Figure 5.6). The planned order is used to request that the company produce a specified quantity of goods. It is similar to a purchase requisition, which we discussed in Chapter 3. The difference is that a purchase requisition is used for materials purchased from a vendor, whereas a planned order is used for materials made within the company. In our example, the source of the planned order is the warehouse because SSB has adopted a make-to-stock strategy; the warehouse wants to increase the stock of skateboards. Under a make-to-order strategy, a company may create planned orders to fill specific customer orders rather than to restock

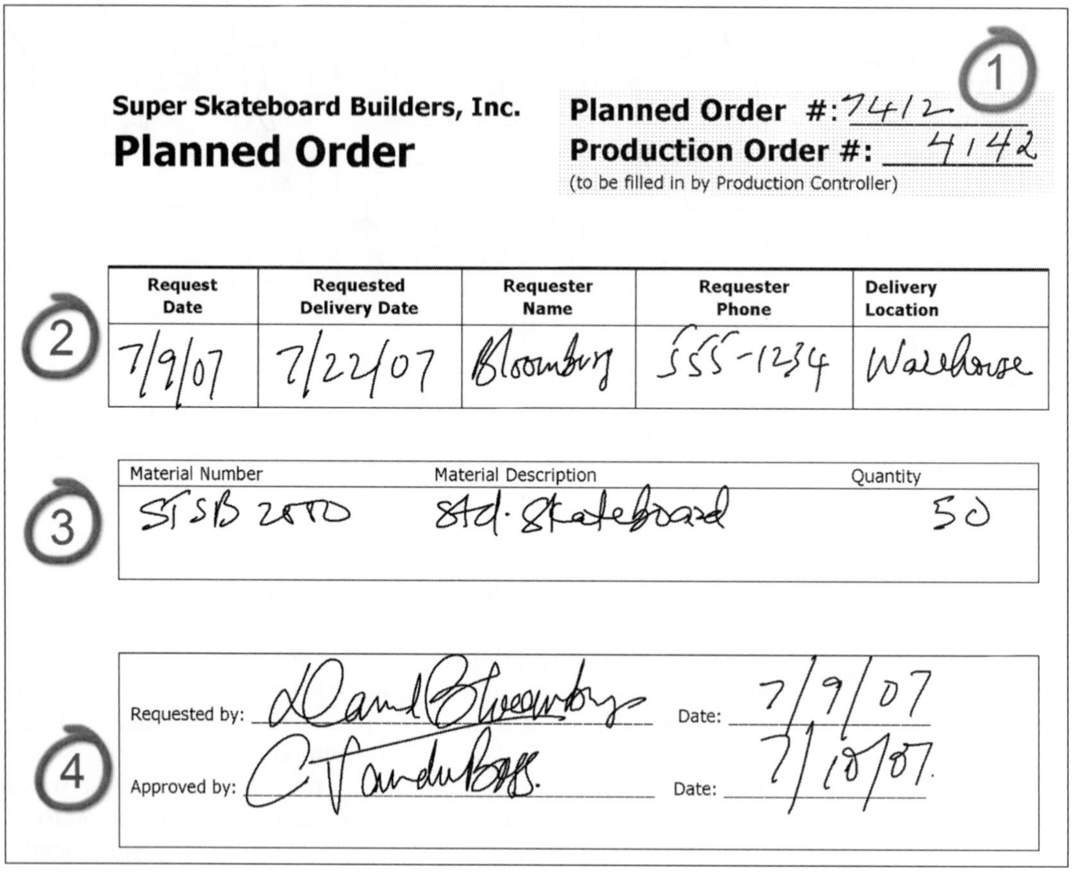

Super Skateboard Builders, Inc.

Planned Order

Planned Order #: 7412

Production Order #: 4142

(to be filled in by Production Controller)

Request Date	Requested Delivery Date	Requester Name	Requester Phone	Delivery Location
7/9/07	7/22/07	Bloomberg	555-1234	Warehouse

Material Number	Material Description	Quantity
SSSB 2000	Std. Skateboard	50

Requested by: David Bloomberg Date: 7/9/07

Approved by: C VanderBos Date: 7/10/07

Figure 5.6 Planned order

inventory. Many planned orders may be submitted from different parts of the organization in response to stock requirements in different warehouses or multiple customer orders. All the planned orders are received by the person responsible for production in the organization, the **production controller**.

In the SSB example in Figure 5.6, the planned order is for 50 standard skateboards (area 3). This order was requested by David Bloomberg in the warehouse on July 9 (area 2). He has requested that the skateboards be available by July 22 (area 2).

Production Order

Planned orders are eventually translated into **production orders** (Figure 5.7) by the production controller, who is responsible for scheduling production in the various production facilities. A production order provides written authorization to the shop floor to produce the stated quantity of products. Multiple planned orders may be consolidated into a single production order or a planned order may be divided into many production orders, depending on the quantity requested and the production capacity available in the different plants.

In our example, the planned order for 50 skateboards is sent to Catherine VanderBos, the plant manager, who fulfills the role of the production controller at SSB. She either approves or denies the order. She bases her decision on a variety

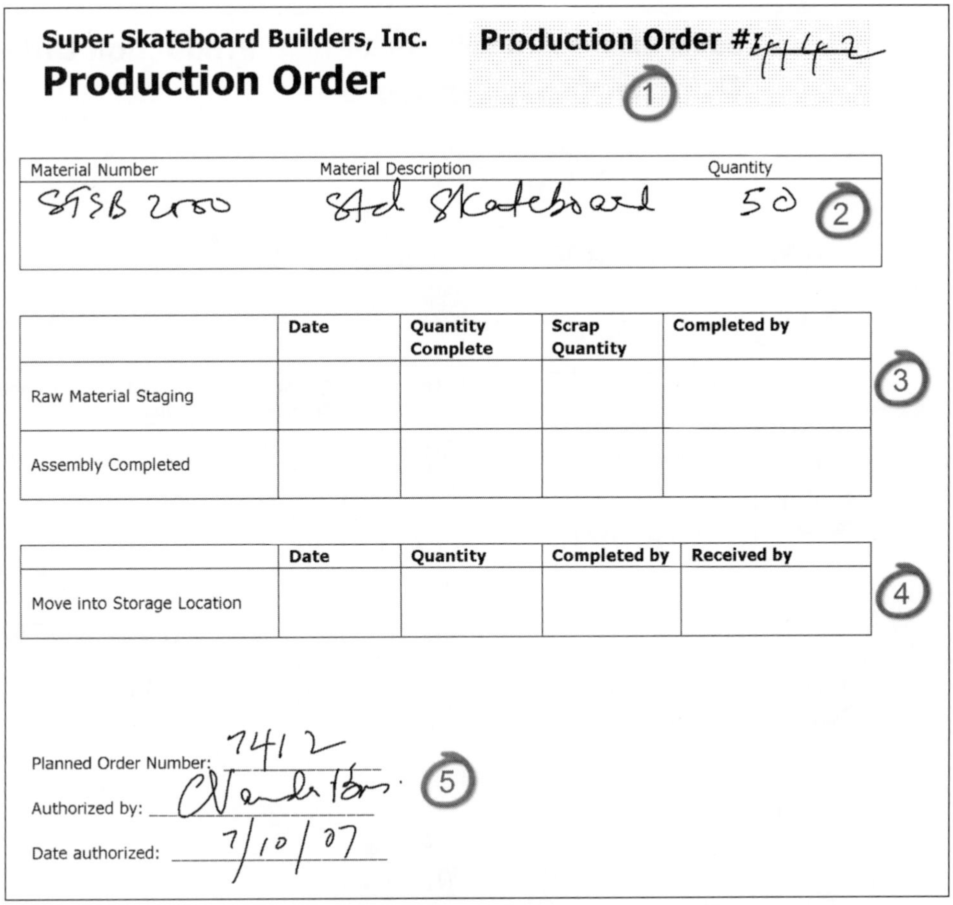

Super Skateboard Builders, Inc.
Production Order

Production Order #*4142* ①

Material Number	Material Description	Quantity
STSB 2000	*Std Skateboard*	*50* ②

	Date	Quantity Complete	Scrap Quantity	Completed by	
Raw Material Staging					③
Assembly Completed					

	Date	Quantity	Completed by	Received by	
Move into Storage Location					④

Planned Order Number: *7412*

Authorized by: *C Vanderhorn* ⑤

Date authorized: *7/10/07*

Figure 5.7 Production order—initial state

of factors such as the availability of resources (e.g., workstations and labor) and whether other planned orders are competing for these resources. In the interests of simplicity, we will not discuss how she makes this decision. We will simply assume that she approves the planned order.

Catherine begins by assigning a number to the planned order (7412; see area 1 in Figure 5.6). Next she creates a production order (Figure 5.7) and assigns a production order number (4142 in area 1). She also adds this number to the planned order for tracking purposes. The production order indicates that 50 standard skateboards have been authorized for production (area 2). It includes the planned order number as well as the authorization date and signature (area 5). At this point, the areas in the document related to the steps in the routing (material staging, assembly, and movement into storage location) are empty (areas 3 and 4). A copy of the updated planned order is sent back to David, for his records. David will file this copy and discard the copy of the original planned order from his files.

Later in the process, in the "create products" step, the rest of the production order is completed (Figure 5.8). In our example, only three steps in the product routing (see Figure 5.4) are tracked (see areas 3 and 4 in Figure 5.8): (1) the initial material staging, (2) the completion of the assembly of skateboards, and (3) moving the skateboards into storage. It is fairly common to track only key steps

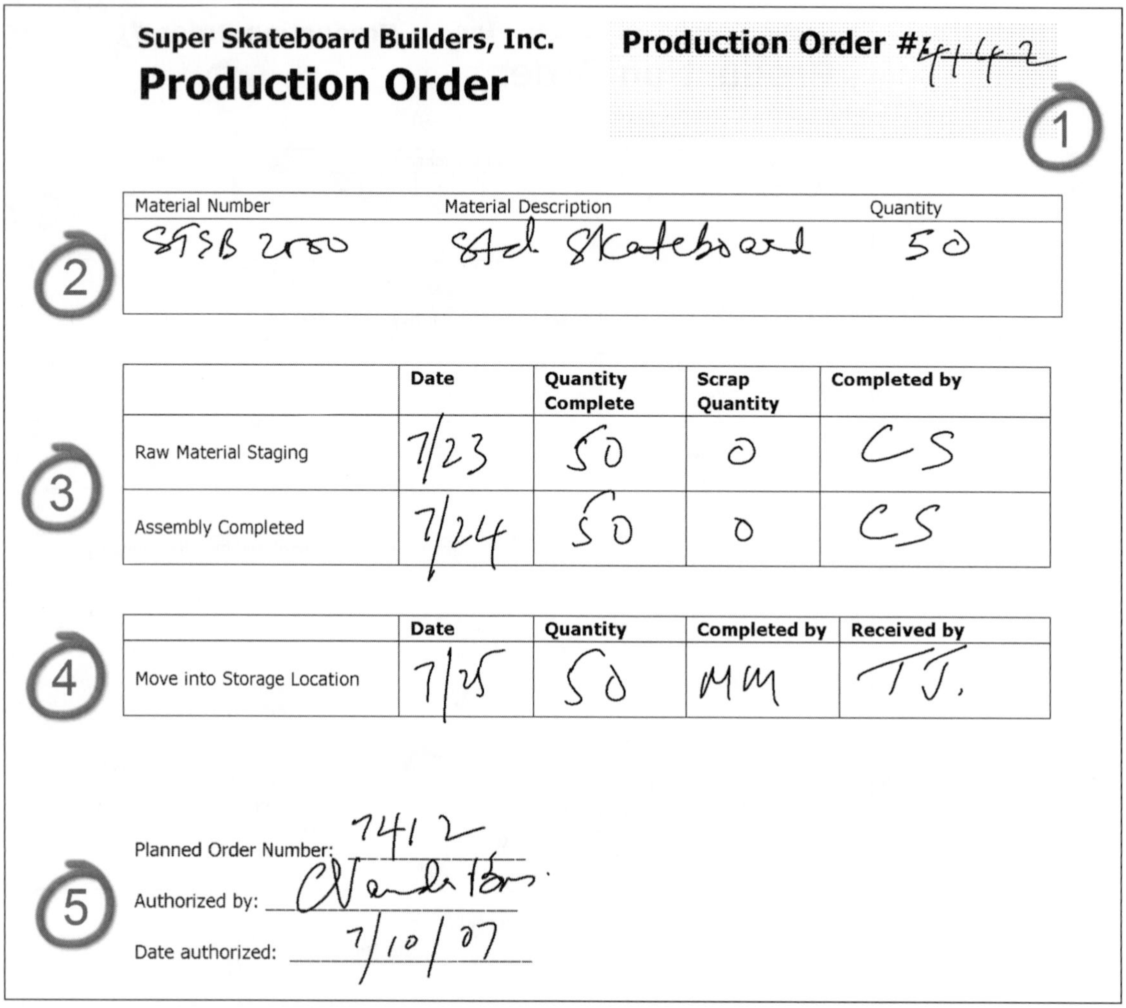

Figure 5.8 Production order—completed state

in the routing. Oftentimes the effort needed to track the process in greater detail is difficult to justify. Figure 5.8 indicates that Charlie Skivers (CS) completed the material staging on July 23 and the production on July 24. Later, Mark McKendry will complete the final part of the production order when he delivers the finished skateboards to Tim in the warehouse. We discuss this step later in the chapter.

Material Withdrawal Slip

When production is authorized, another document, called a **material withdrawal slip** (Figure 5.9), is also created. The material withdrawal slip includes a list of all the materials needed to produce the quantity of finished goods stated in the production order. This document authorizes the warehouse to release or issue the materials to the shop floor when it is ready to start production.

In our example, the material withdrawal slip includes the production order number and the quantity authorized at the top of the document (area 1). It identifies the eight materials needed to make the skateboards, the quantities needed per skateboard, and the total quantity needed to complete the entire order (area 3). The

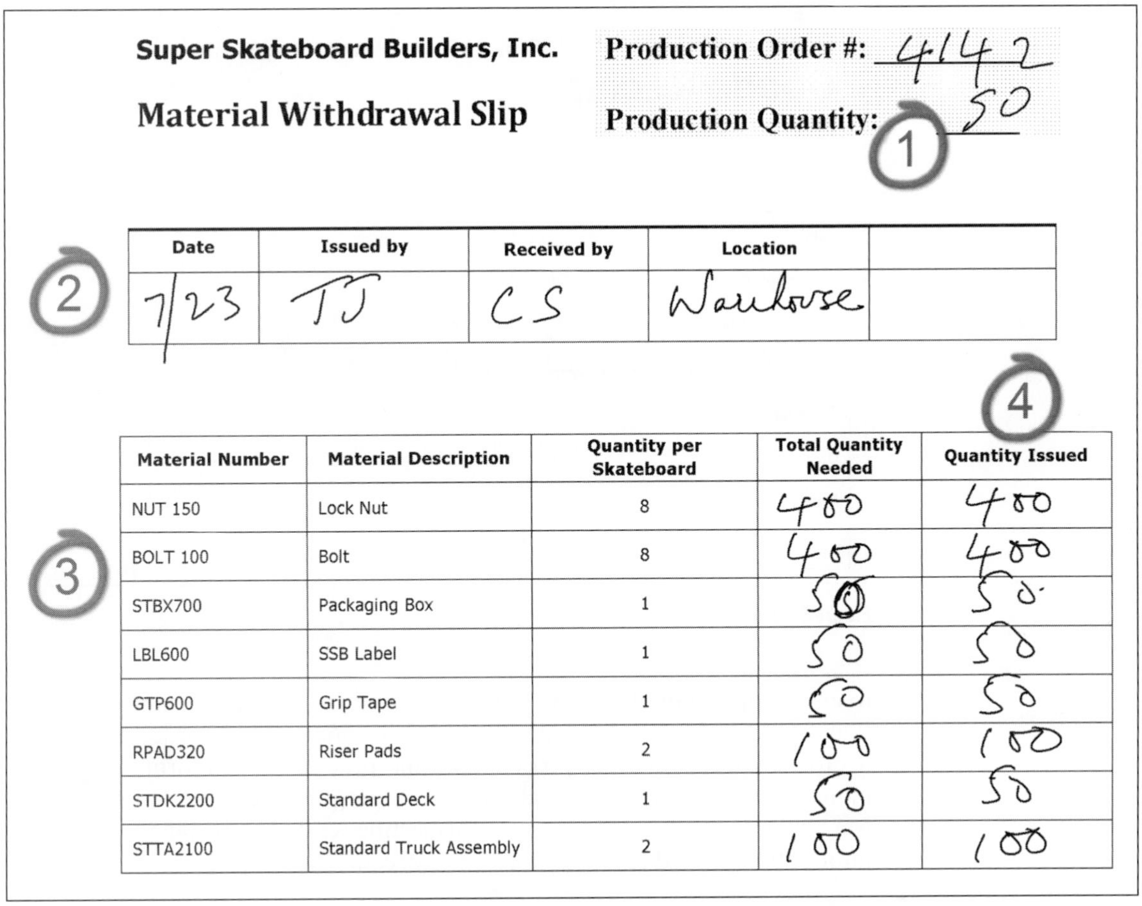

Super Skateboard Builders, Inc.			Production Order #: _4142_	
Material Withdrawal Slip			Production Quantity: _50_ ①	

Date	Issued by	Received by	Location	
7/23	TJ	C S	Warehouse	

② ④

Material Number	Material Description	Quantity per Skateboard	Total Quantity Needed	Quantity Issued
NUT 150	Lock Nut	8	400	400
BOLT 100	Bolt	8	400	400
STBX700	Packaging Box	1	50	50
LBL600	SSB Label	1	50	50
GTP600	Grip Tape	1	50	50
RPAD320	Riser Pads	2	100	100
STDK2200	Standard Deck	1	50	50
STTA2100	Standard Truck Assembly	2	100	100

③

Figure 5.9 Material withdrawal slip

slip indicates that materials were issued to Charlie Skivers by Tim Jones on July 23 (area 2). At this time, the quantity issued column (area 4) is updated to reflect the actual quantity that was issued.

Goods Receipt Document

When Mark delivers the 50 completed skateboards to Tim in the warehouse in the final step of the production process, Tim will complete a **goods receipt document** (Figure 5.10), which serves as a record for the warehouse. The document indicates that Mark delivered the skateboards to Tim on 7/25/07 against production order #4142. While Tim completes the goods receipt document, Mark completes the production order document (area 4 of Figure 5.8) for the records maintained in the shop floor.

5.1.6 Information Flow

Like procurement and fulfillment, production involves both instance-level and process-level information. As we discussed in Chapter 3, the procurement process uses instance-level information to monitor each individual purchase order and process-level information to monitor the aggregate steps in the procurement process

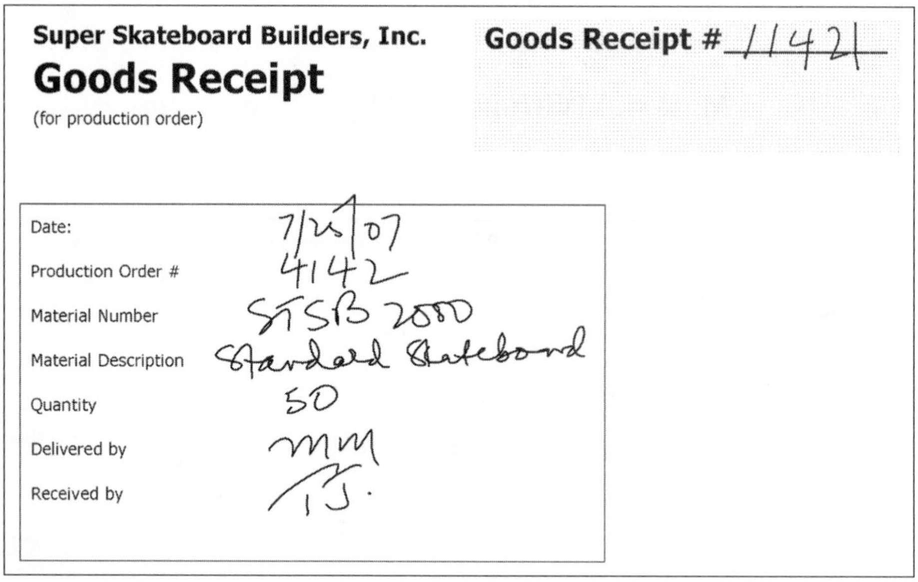
Super Skateboard Builders, Inc.

Goods Receipt #1142

Goods Receipt

(for production order)

Date:	7/25/07
Production Order #	4142
Material Number	STSB 2000
Material Description	Standard Skateboard
Quantity	50
Delivered by	MM
Received by	TJ.

Figure 5.10 Goods receipt document

to ensure optimum efficiency. In the fulfillment process the instance-level information regarding each sales order was used to monitor each order and shipment as it progressed through the process, and the process-level information was used to monitor and analyze the overall fulfillment process to ensure that customer orders were being processed efficiently. In this section we discuss instance and process level information related to the production process.

Instance-Level Information

Instance-level production information is concerned with a single planned order and its progress as it goes through the production process. Much of the information is concerned with the status of the order. Has it been approved? Have the requested materials been produced? In other words, in which stage of the process is the order?

As was true of the fulfillment and procurement processes, in a manual environment the answers to these questions are obtained by retrieving and inspecting the data contained in the various documents. In the case of SSB, David Bloomberg wants to know if the 50 skateboards he requested have been produced. To acquire this information, he will first retrieve the planned order from his files. If his copy of the planned order is the one that Catherine sent to him, David knows that the order was approved because it will have a production order number on it. He will then call Catherine, give her the production order number, and inquire about the status of the order.

Catherine will look for the production order in the shop floor files. If she finds it, then it will either be in its original state (Figure 5.7) or in the completed state (Figure 5.8). If she does not find it, then the most likely reason is that it is out on the shop floor, meaning that the order is being produced. (Of course, it is also possible that the paperwork has been misplaced.) Catherine will confirm this by going to the workstations and asking if they are working on the particular order. In either case, she will then communicate the status of the project to David.

Process-Level Information

Process-level information is concerned with the production process as a whole, across multiple instances, over time. It incorporates data from all the documents related to multiple executions of the production process. Companies use this information to determine how well the process as a whole is functioning. It addresses questions such as:

- What is the average time needed to make a skateboard?
- What is the average time needed to complete each step in the routing?
- What percent of the production orders are completed on time? What percent are delayed?
- What is the cause of the delays in completing production orders?
- What percent of the skateboards fail final inspection and have to be scrapped? Why do they fail?

As with the other processes, this aggregated information is very difficult to compile in a manual environment because it has to be extracted from various documents and compiled by hand. As we might expect, then, production increasingly relies on enterprise systems (ES) to make the system function more efficiently. We address the use of ES in the final section of this chapter.

▶ 5.2 ROLE OF ENTERPRISE SYSTEMS IN THE PRODUCTION PROCESS

As with procurement and fulfillment, enterprise systems facilitate production by helping the company to execute the process, capture and store data, and monitor its operations. Storing all the process data in a common database enables the company to obtain information about either a specific production order (instance) or the production process as a whole over a period of time. In this section we focus on the ways in which an ES can contribute to production. We also illustrate the role an ES in Figure 5.11.

5.2.1 Execute the Process

The ES helps the people involved perform their part of the production process. It performs this function by storing all the data associated with the process in a common database and by helping the different persons and functional areas involved in the process communicate with one another.

Request Production

The simple production process described in this chapter starts with David Bloomberg in the warehouse. As we explained, David has to monitor the quantity of skateboards in the warehouse to determine if it has dropped below some predetermined level. In the manual process, David must observe and keep track of the inventory himself. In contrast, an enterprise system can provide David with the information he needs. As one option, David can periodically retrieve an inventory report that indicates the number of skateboards currently in the warehouse (area 1 in Figure 5.11). This report helps David determine whether more skateboards are needed.

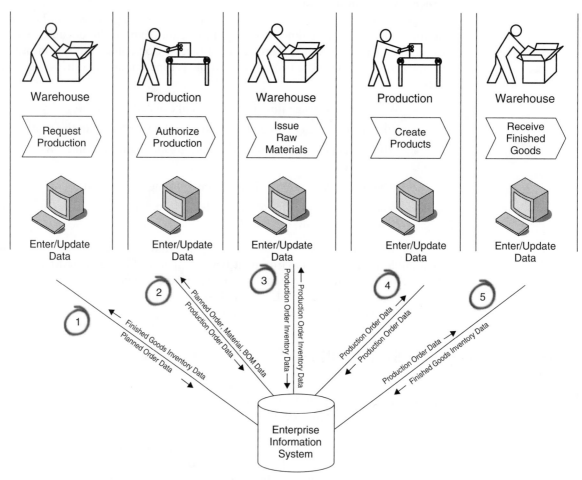

Figure 5.11 Enterprise systems in the production process

Another option is to configure the system so that it automatically notifies David when the inventory levels drop below the predetermined quantity. In fact, a highly automated system could automatically generate the planned order when more inventory is needed.

SSB has configured their system so that David has to create the planned order himself. He will log into the system and access the program to create a planned order (Figure 5.12). However, David does *not* have to provide all the data required in the planned order. He needs to provide only the material number (STSB2000 in area 1), the location (PT00 in area 1), the quantity (50 in area 2), and the date needed (finish date in area 3). The system has access to all the necessary master data, such as the bill of material and routing. In a manual environment, David's signature is needed to prove that he requested the production. With an ES, such proof is not necessary because the system automatically identifies the person who is logged in, and the login information is sufficient proof of identify. When David is satisfied with the data in the planned order, he will save the order. At this point the system will generate a planned order number and will store the data in the common database, as indicated in area 1 of Figure 5.11

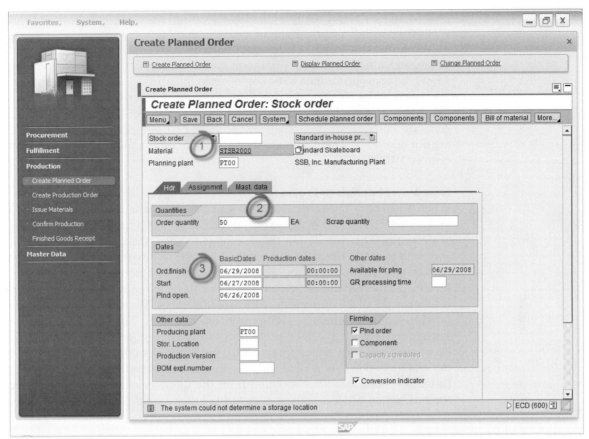

Figure 5.12   Creating a planned order in SAP® ERP
Source: Copyright SAP AG 2008

Authorize Production

After David has created the planned order, Catherine, the production controller, must be made aware of its existence so that she can act on it. An ES provides Catherine with the same basic options as David. That is, she can log into the system periodically to retrieve a list of available planned orders and act on them, or the system can notify her each time a new planned order is created. In highly automated environments, the ES can automatically authorize production whenever certain conditions are met. Manual authorization is required only if exceptions to these conditions occur.

SSB has configured their system so that Catherine must log into the system to determine if planned orders exist for her to act on. She will authorize production by creating a production order based on the data contained in an existing planned order. In addition, the system will provide other relevant data such as BOM and the availability of raw materials (area 2 in Figure 5.11). Catherine will use this information to authorize the production, reject it, or postpone it. When the system retrieves the planned order, it will automatically check to see if the needed raw materials are available, and it will examine the work centers to determine when the needed capacity will be available. These capabilities allow SSB to modify their process to be more responsive to their needs. They also help SSB to integrate production with their procurement and fulfillment processes.

In a manual system, Catherine would have to create a production order by writing in all the necessary information on the appropriate form. In contrast, an ES allows the appropriate data to be copied from the planned order because it stores all these data in the common database automatically. Catherine can modify any of the data, such as quantities and start or finish dates, as needed. The ES will automatically generate a production order number. As in the case of the planned order, signatures are not necessary. These data are then stored in the common database for later use (Figure 5.11, area 2).

Issue Raw Materials to Production Order
When Charles in the shop floor logs into the enterprise system, he can see if an authorized production order exists. If one does exist, he will begin making the skateboards. The first step in the routing is to stage the needed raw material. To complete this task, Charles will need to obtain the raw material from the warehouse. In a manual environment, he would have to present the material withdrawal slip to Tim (in the warehouse) as authorization to issue the material. When using an ES, however, all Charles needs is the order number. He will go to the warehouse, provide the order number, and request the materials. Tim will then log into the system, retrieve the specified production order, and request the system to display list of materials to be issued (Figure 5.13) for the production order. This list displays the materials that are needed (area 1) to produce as well as the quantity needed (area 2). These data are calculated from the quantity of skateboards specified in the production order and the associated bill of material. If the BOM changes, the

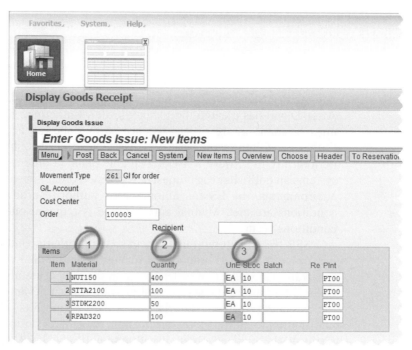

Figure 5.13 Goods issue for production order in SAP® ERP
Source: Copyright SAP AG 2008

system will always have the most up-to-date data to determine what materials are needed. In a manual environment this process is more problematic, and it functions properly only if the changes have been communicated to the production controller, the warehouse, and the shop floor. Given the poor communication and coordination among functions that frequently characterizes a manual environment, it is not unusual for the wrong materials to be issued to production orders.

Tim retrieves the needed raw materials from the shelves, gives them to Charles, and verifies the data in the system. If the quantity issued is different from the quantity indicated in the system, Tim will change the data in the system accordingly (Figure 5.13, area 2). In addition, he will verify that the storage location from where the materials are retrieved (area 3) is correct; if not, he will update the data in the system. He will then save the data in the system. The system automatically includes the date of the goods issue ("today") and the name of the employee who issued the material (Tim, because he is the one logged into the system). The updated production order, material withdrawal data, and inventory data are now stored in the system.

Create (Assemble) Products

Charles then takes the materials and prepares them for use in work center 200, the staging area in the shop floor. Once he has completed this task, he will log into the system, retrieve the production order, confirm that the staging is complete, and provide the quantity staged and quantity scrapped (discarded).

Next, Charles completes the assembly and inspection steps. He then logs into the system once again and confirms that he has completed these steps. As in the staging step, he provides the quantities of finished goods, and the system automatically includes the other data.

Recall from our discussion of the manual process that organizations often do not track progress at each step in the assembly process. In the manual environment, we included tracking (confirmation) at three steps—raw material staging, assembly completion, and movement to storage location (see Figure 5.8). In our example involving an ES, we will only include one confirmation—the final confirmation that all steps in the production are completed. To indicate this, Mark will log into the system and access the program to confirm production and provide the production order number. The system will provide a form (Figure 5.14) that includes the order number (area 1) and a place to enter the quantity produced (area 2). Because sufficient materials were issued to make 50 skateboards, if the quantity produced is less than 50, then Mark must indicate how many skateboards were discarded (scrapped) or need additional work (rework) to be of satisfactory quality. In addition, Mark will provide start and end times for the steps needed to produce the skateboards (area 3).

Finally, Mark moves the finished goods to storage. In the manual process, he would have to complete area 4 of the production order (Figure 5.8). With an enterprise system, however, Mark need not explicitly complete this step. The system will automatically complete this step when Tim receives the goods in the warehouse. This step is explained next.

Receive Finished Goods into Storage

Mark takes the 50 skateboards just completed to Tim in the warehouse and provides him with the production order number. Tim retrieves the production order and records a goods receipt against that production order (Figure 5.15). The goods

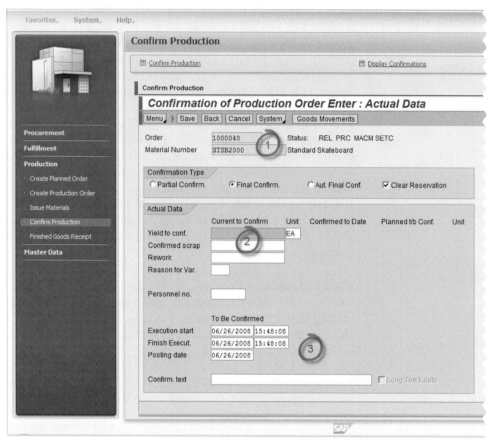

Figure 5.14 Production confirmation in SAP® ERP
Source: Copyright SAP AG 2008

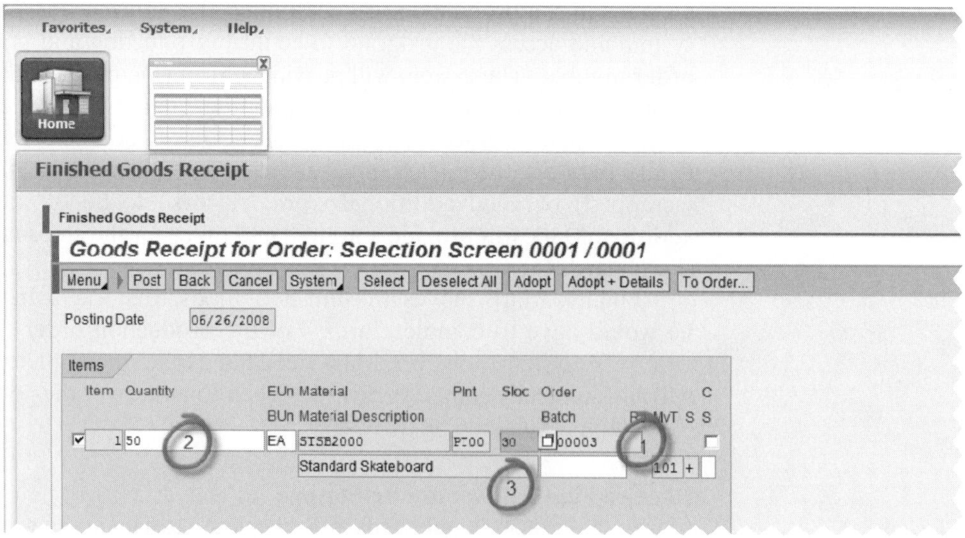

Figure 5.15 Goods receipt for production order in SAP® ERP
Source: Copyright SAP AG 2008

receipt document will display the production order number (area 1), and Tim will provide the quantity received (area 2) and the location where the materials are stored (area 3). The system automatically adds the date and notes that Tim received the goods. The other data in the goods receipt document—material number and description—are obtained automatically from the production order.

5.2.2 Capture and Store Process Data

At this point the role of enterprise systems in capturing and processing data should be apparent. In a manual system, the completion of process steps and the recording of the data in the documents are not linked. That is, completing the document associated with a process step is not essential to completion of the step. As a consequence, if the person completing the step fails to record the information or is too busy to do so, the data in the documents may not reflect the reality of the process. For example, if Catherine provides verbal authorization for production or Charles completes production and neither one remembers to update the production order, then neither the fact that they completed their steps nor the data associated with the steps will be recorded. An inquiry into the status of the planned order that initiated the process will indicate that the order has not yet been approved, when in fact the production has been completed.

In contrast, when using an ES, the system is critical to the completion of the steps, and the data are automatically recorded. Process steps cannot be completed without interacting with the system. The physical steps and the system are intertwined. For example, Catherine cannot authorize production without retrieving a planned order from the system. When she approves it, this fact is immediately recorded. She cannot provide a verbal or written authorization because the warehouse will not release the raw material if the authorization is not recorded in the system.

5.2.3 Monitor the process

As in the cases of procurement and fulfillment, enterprise systems allow organizations to easily obtain information about the state of a specific order as well as about the process over time. We examine both functions in this section.

Instance-Level Information

At the instance level, enterprise systems provide status information, typically about the status of a specific order at a point in time. Consider again the steps in the production process described earlier. David needs to know how many standard skateboards are in inventory so that he can determine if SSB must produce more. David will log into the system and request an inventory status report that will show how many skateboards are in stock.

Several days after creating a planned order requesting production of 50 skateboards, David wants to know what the status of that order is. He logs into the system and retrieves a stock requirements list (Figure 5.16). He notes that there are 10 skateboards in inventory (area 1), and three production orders have been scheduled to produce a total of 80 skateboards (area 2).

Next he will drill down to a specific production order to determine its status (Figure 5.17). He concludes that production has been completed because the order displays productions dates (area 1) and confirms that 50 skateboards have been produced (confirmed quantity in area 2). David further notes that the delivered

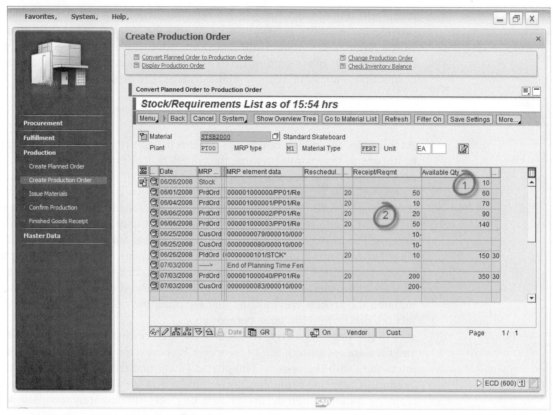

Figure 5.16 Stock requirements list in SAP® ERP
Source: Copyright SAP AG 2008

quantity is zero, indicating that the goods have not been received into storage (the final step in the production process—see Figure 5.5).

Process-Level Information

At the process level, an enterprise system can provide information about how well the process is performing over time. Figure 5.18 provides information about the production of standard skateboards during the month of January. It shows that there were 7 orders in January (area 1), of which 3 were delayed, for an on-time completion percent of 57%. Each order took just under 3 days to complete, and each skateboard took just over 9 minutes to make. Recall from our earlier discussion that the standard (expected) time to produce one skateboard is 9 minutes. Thus, the process appears to be running as expected. However, it is necessary to look more closely into the three delayed orders.

The bottom of Figure 5.18 (area 2) shows some detail for each order, and the graph (area 3) summarizes the status by the stage in the production process. Orders #7414 and #7418 are delayed in a particular step in the process, whereas #7417 is delayed because SSB is waiting for materials. More details for each can be obtained by "drilling down" and retrieving the needed information. It is worth noting that, in the case of Order #7417, the company appears to have run short of the needed raw materials. This shortage indicates a problem not with the production process but with the procurement process. Although we have discussed the three

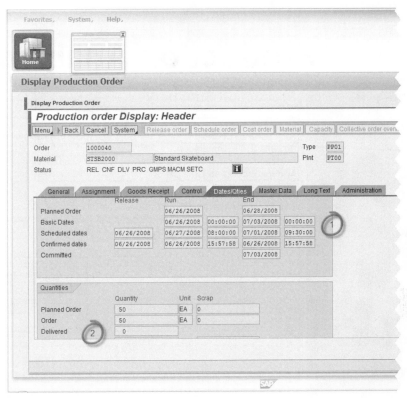

Figure 5.17 Production order status in SAP® ERP
Source: Copyright SAP AG 2008

processes—procurement, fulfillment, and production—as separate processes, in reality they are highly integrated and dependent on one another. We discuss integrated processes in greater detail in Chapter 6.

▶ 5.3 EXERCISE USING SIMULATED SAP® ERP

As in the case of the previous chapters, it is now time for you to experience an enterprise system in action using a simulated SAP® ERP environment.

Go to WileyPLUS and complete the exercises for this chapter. The exercises consist of three parts, two exercises and a short quiz. The first exercise will guide you through the steps in the production process, whereas in the second one you will complete the steps on your own, without any guidance.

The exercises will take you through the following steps that have been discussed in this chapter:

1. Create a planned order
2. Convert the planned order to a production order
3. Issue materials to the production order
4. Confirm production
5. Move finished materials to inventory

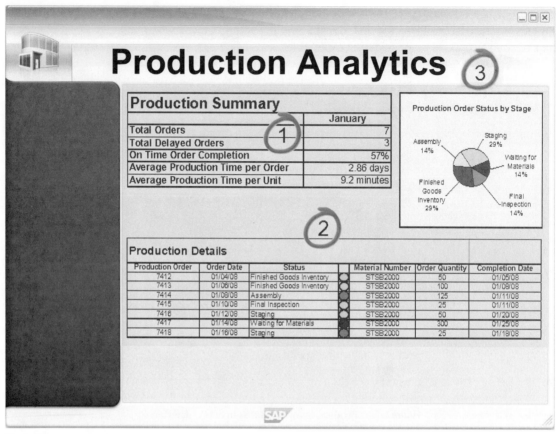

Figure 5.18   Production analytics
Source: Copyright SAP AG 2008

The final part of the exercise is a short quiz that will test your knowledge of the production process. Your instructor will direct you to the location of the quiz. After you have completed the quiz, the system will grade it and send your score to your professor's grade book. You may view your score in the gradebook tab of WileyPLUS.

As before, please pay attention to what you are doing and understand why the actions are necessary to execute the process. You may repeat these exercises as often as needed to thoroughly understand the production process and how an enterprise system supports it.

▶ CHAPTER SUMMARY

In this chapter we explained a very simple production process, involving a few key steps. In reality, production is far more complex and may involve many more steps. However, the purpose here is to focus on the fundamentals. A production process begins with a need for materials. The need is either due to a specific customer order, when a make-to-order strategy is in use, or due to a need to increase inventory of materials on hand, when a make-to-stock strategy is used. In either case, this need is presented in the form of a planned order. A planned order must be approved by the production controller and, once approved, results in a production order. A production order is a commitment to produce and authorizes the warehouse to release materials needed to produce the needed products. It also authorizes the shop floor to commence production. The materials are then issued from the warehouse to the production order, at which point the production can begin. Once production is complete, it is noted (confirmation) and the materials produced are moved into storage.

An enterprise system facilitates the production process by capturing and storing all the data in a common database. It reduces the need to communicate using paper documents by the use of electronic documents. In some cases, the system can automate the communication as well as some of the steps in the process.

Enterprise systems can remove many of the redundancies and delays inherent in a manual process and can alleviate problems related to coordination and visibility. Problems are detected sooner and with fewer obstacles, enabling people to respond to them more promptly and effectively.

► KEY TERMS

assembling	make-to-order	process manufacturing	production orders
bill of materials	make-to-stock	product design	work centers
discrete manufacturing	manufacturing	product routings	
engineering drawing	material withdrawal slip	production capacity	
goods receipt document	planned order	production controller	

► REVIEW QUESTIONS

1. Explain the difference between make-to-order and make-to-stock strategies.

2. Explain the key steps in a basic production process.

3. Briefly describe the key documents in the production process in terms of their role in the process.

► ASSIGNMENTS

1. The production process described in this chapter is deliberately very simple. Based on your experiences or by talking to someone in a local company, define and describe a more complex production process in terms of the physical, document, and data flows. What functions of the organizations will be involved in this process?

2. This chapter provides some examples of instance level and process level information. Identify two more examples of each type of information and explain what data will be needed to generate this information. What is the source of these data?

3. Identify some of the key problems associated with the manual, or paper-based, production process. How does an enterprise system eliminate or reduce the impact of these problems?

4. SSB has a need to produce 100 standard skateboards to replenish inventory. Create all the documents necessary to document the process used to produce these materials. You can search the Internet for examples of the documents included in this chapter or you can create them using a word processor.

CHAPTER 6

Integrated Processes

Learning Objectives

After completing this chapter you will be able to:

▶ Define end-to-end processes that integrate the fulfillment, procurement, and production processes.

▶ Describe the steps in a fully integrated end-to-end integrated process.

▶ Explain how enterprise systems support end-to-end integrated processes.

▶ Describe additional intracompany processes and business processes that occur between companies.

In the preceding three chapters, we explained how the key processes in an organization—procurement, fulfillment, and production—work in terms of the physical, data, document, and information flows, and how an enterprise system (ES) supports these processes. We explained that although the individual steps in these processes are executed in different parts of an organization, they are all parts of an integrated business process. Now that you understand procurement, fulfillment, and production as stand-alone processes, we will tie these three processes together into a single, **integrated process**. In addition, we will briefly describe some of the other processes that typically occur within and among organizations.

Procurement, fulfillment, and production, as well as the integrated process to be discussed in this chapter, are all **intracompany processes**. That is, most, if not all, of the steps occur within the boundaries of a single organization. In Chapter 2 we introduced **intercompany processes**, such as supply chain management (SCM) and customer relationship management (CRM), that connect processes across two or more organizations. Although this book focuses on intracompany processes, we will end this chapter with a very brief discussion of some of the most important intercompany processes. For many companies, especially large global companies, thinking internally is no longer sufficient. Rather, companies must think in terms of how multiple entities—customers, suppliers, manufacturers, and financial institutions—operate as a network of businesses that are highly dependent on one another.

Recently, many large and small companies have begun to transform their business networks to take advantage of the special capabilities of their partners and customers. Companies are using ES to break up their traditional business processes and divide them throughout their network of partners and customers. Typical tasks that a company traditionally would carry out on its own, such as R&D and payment processing, are now performed by a company's partners. For example, Procter & Gamble (P&G) has enjoyed tremendous success creating a network of partners to help source and develop new product ideas and improvements. Using a collaborative ES, this network has created a large Internet repository that allows P&G to post requirements for new product capabilities or features while enabling thousands of partners to submit proposals for the solutions. If one of the partners has a solution that fits P&G's needs, the company licenses that technology, patent, or idea so they can get the new product into the market as quickly as possible. This transformation of P&G's research unit into an "idea-sourcing" team has been so comprehensive that nearly half of P&G's new products in 2007 contained elements that originated outside the company. For example, P&G was looking for new ways to package and market Pringles potato chips by printing trivia questions and funny quotations on each individual chip with edible ink. Rather than spend several years and several million dollars to develop the ink and technology to print on the potato chips, they were able to source the technology from a small bakery in Italy—at a fraction of the cost and time it would have taken to develop it themselves.[1]

▶ 6.1 INTEGRATED PROCESSES

The preceding chapters discussed procurement, fulfillment, and production in very simplistic terms to make them easier to understand. When we discussed fulfillment, for example, we assumed that the products ordered by the customer were in stock and available to ship. We did not address a situation in which the products were unavailable. In addition, we were using a sell-from-stock strategy so that we didn't have to deal with issues related to production. When we discussed production in Chapter 5, we made the same assumptions concerning the necessary raw materials as we did regarding finished products in the preceding chapters.

In the real world, however, the three key processes are actually tightly integrated. Consider, for example, what happens if a customer orders some standard skateboards (which SSB assembles in the production process), and there are no finished goods in stock. In this case, SSB starts the fulfillment process normally, but it must suspend the process after it determines that there are insufficient finished goods to fulfill the sales order.

In this case, a check of inventory to determine if the needed skateboards are in stock serves as the **decision point** that SSB uses to start the production process. Once the production process is complete and the skateboards have been produced, the fulfillment process can continue normally. However, now consider what happens if SSB has insufficient raw materials to manufacture the needed skateboards. This determination serves as another decision point. If there are insufficient raw materials to produce the needed skateboards, then, just as SSB previously suspended the fulfillment process until it produced the necessary skateboards, it must now suspend the production process until it procures the needed raw materials. When the raw materials have been received in the warehouse toward the end of the procurement process, then the production process can be resumed.

Going further, when we discussed the processes in the previous chapters, we first explained how they are performed in a manual, paper-based environment. We then concluded each chapter by demonstrating how the process is executed with the use of an ES. In this chapter, we will not discuss the paper-based environment but will focus exclusively on the use of ES. The only paper documents will be those involving external entities, such as customers and suppliers.

---

[1]Huston, L., & Sakkab, N. (2006). Connect and develop. *Harvard Business Review*, *84*(3), 58–66.

Before we proceed, however, we first need to revisit some of the assumptions that we made in our discussions of the procurement, fulfillment, and production processes. Remember that we treated them as independent processes. When we discussed the procurement process, for example, we assumed a procure-to-stock strategy. Under this strategy, materials are purchased and placed into inventory. The procurement process is triggered by a need to increase the inventory of either trading goods or raw materials. The production process is triggered by a need to increase the inventory of finished goods. It employs a make-to-stock strategy with the assumption that the materials needed for production are always available. The materials produced into finished goods are later used during the fulfillment process to fill customer orders using the sell-from-stock strategy. These strategies explicitly separate the three processes, using inventory as the key mechanism for linking them. Although this approach simplifies the processes, it also increases costs due to the need to maintain sufficient levels of inventory as well as the planning needed to determine when additional inventory is needed.

Alternative strategies for procurement and production are procure-to-order and make-to-order, respectively. Under these strategies, production of materials is triggered by a customer order (for materials produced in-house), whereas procurement is triggered either by insufficient supplies of materials needed to complete production or by a customer order for trading goods. Thus, the three processes are very tightly integrated, and the company maintains no inventory. Instead, it includes the lead times for procurement when it determines a delivery date to the customer. By not maintaining inventory, the company reduces its inventory costs. However, the delivery time to the customer is increased, which can be detrimental to the company. In addition, these strategies involve procuring or producing just enough for the company to fill the customer order. The problem with this approach is that it may be more economical to order or produce larger quantities, for example, due to price discounts from vendors for large purchases.

In sum, then, neither of the two sets of strategies described is ideal. For this reason, companies tend to utilize a combination of the two. In our discussion of integrated processes in this chapter, we will use the make-/procure-to-stock strategies. However, we will make or procure goods or materials in **fixed order quantities**, which may be greater than what the customer ordered or what production requires. Fixed order quantities are more economical than variable order quantities because they have been predetermined to minimize costs, but they also lead to the accumulation of some inventory. Determining optimal fixed order quantities is a complex process that is covered in operations management courses and is beyond the scope of this book. For our purposes we will assume that SSB has determined the optimal quantities using appropriate methods.

▶ 6.2 INTEGRATED PROCESS EXECUTION

This integrated process is depicted in Figure 6.1. The steps in the figure are essentially the same as those in the three individual processes. However, there are a few differences. Perhaps the most fundamental difference is that the integrated process includes points at which inventory must be checked and a decision made. These are the decision points briefly explained earlier and serve to determine which of two paths the process will follow. If there is sufficient inventory, then the process continues; if not, then the process forks to a different path. The concepts of multiple

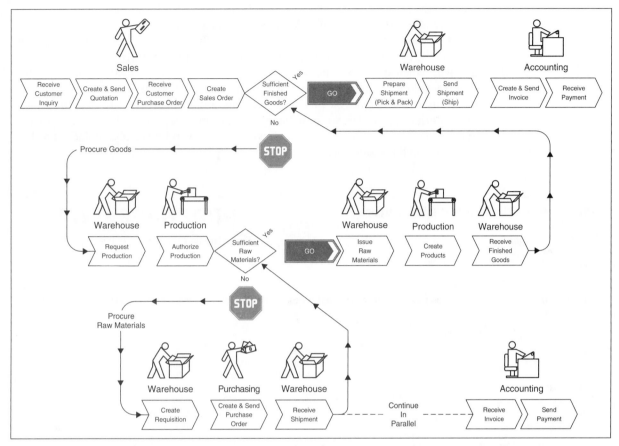

Figure 6.1 Integrated, end-to-end process

paths and branching or forking are very common in business processes. We did not include them in previous chapters because we wanted to keep the discussion simple.

In our following discussion of the integrated process, we will refer you to previous chapters for a review of most of the steps. We will focus primarily on the additional steps related to checking inventory and determining which path to take for the subsequent steps. It will be helpful to review the SSB organizational chart from Chapter 2 to recall the roles of the various people involved in the process.

6.2.1 The Fulfillment Process: Initial Steps

The integrated process begins with the first steps of the fulfillment process. A customer submits an inquiry; the company responds with a quotation; the customer then sends a purchase order. In our example, World Wide Skateboard Distributors sends a purchase order to SSB for 100 standard skateboards. Recall from Chapter 4 that Matt, in the sales department, receives the inquiry and prepares the quotation. He also receives the customer purchase order and creates the sales order in the ES. In our fulfillment example in Chapter 4, we had included trading goods. Here we are including standard skateboards, which are assembled in-house. Figure 6.2 shows the purchase order from World Wide Skateboard Distributors.

The warehouse is the next functional area that normally becomes involved in fulfillment. Recall that Tim (warehouse) logs into the ES to retrieve the delivery due list, which displays a list of all orders that are to be prepared for shipment. When we discussed the fulfillment process in Chapter 4, we assumed that the needed materials were in stock. Consequently, Tim simply proceeded to pick and pack the materials. However, we now have an additional step in our integrated process, namely, a decision point to determine whether the warehouse has sufficient finished goods to fulfill the sales order.

World Wide Skateboard Distributors   # PURCHASE ORDER

1229 Westwinde Street
An Arbor, MI, 48109   **Purchase Order Number: 100329**
Phone 734.555.5638 Fax 734.555.55648

THE PURCHASE ORDER NUMBER MUST APPEAR ON ALL RELATED CORRESPONDENCE, SHIPPING DOCUMENTS, AND INVOICES

TO: **SHIP TO:**
Mr. Matt Jones   World Wide Skateboard Distributors
SSB, Inc.   Mid West Warehouse
1 Skateboard Drive   1229 Westwinde Street
Grand Rapids, MI, 49525   Ann Arbor, MI, 48109
616.555.1234   Phone 734.555.5638 Fax 734.555.5648

Purchase Order #	P.O. DATE	Delivery Date	Shipped VIA	F.O.B. Point	Payment Terms
100329	July 1, 2008	July 25, 2008	Ground	Receiving Dock	Net 30

Quantity	Material #	Material Description	Unit Type	Unit Price	Item Total
100	STSB2000	Standard Skateboard	Each	66.00	6,600.00

SUBTOTAL	$ 6,600.00
SALES TAX	Exempt
SHIPPING & HANDLING	Included
OTHER	N/A
ORDER TOTAL	$ 6,600.00

Authorized by: _P. Wilson._   Date 7/1/08
P. Wilson, Purchasing Agent

Figure 6.2   Customer purchase order

6.2.2 Review Inventory of Finished Goods

In a manual environment, someone would physically check the warehouse to determine if there were a sufficient number of finished goods. When using an ES, however, there are several ways to determine inventory status. The simplest method is to retrieve an inventory report from the ES. In our example, Tim (warehouse) does just that, and the resulting report is displayed in Figure 6.3. The report shows the material for which the report is requested (area 1) and the quantity available (area 2). A blank in the "unrestricted use" column indicates that no standard skateboards are currently available.

There are also more sophisticated options for performing an **availability check** for materials. For example, given the integrated nature of an ES and the fact that all the data are stored in a common database, an availability check can be requested automatically when a sales order is created. In this case the ES will display a variation of the inventory report shown in Figure 6.3 along with all the orders for the selected material. A third mechanism is to request a *stock requirements list*, which is displayed in Figure 6.4. A stock requirements list will display all the data associated with the materials, including the available inventory, sales orders, purchase requisitions or orders (for trading goods), and planned or production orders (for manufactured or assembled goods). Our example in Figure 6.4 shows the material (area 1), current inventory (area 2), and the customer order for 100 units (area 3). This stock requirements list will expand as additional steps in the process, associated with the material, are completed.

6.2.3 The Production Process: Initial Steps

Because the desired number of standard skateboards is not available, SSB must produce them to fulfill the sales order. Recall from Chapter 5 that the production process begins with a request for production in the form of a planned order. A planned order can be created by anyone in the organization who wishes to initiate the production process. Planned orders are then reviewed by the production controller and, if appropriate, production is authorized via a production order. In

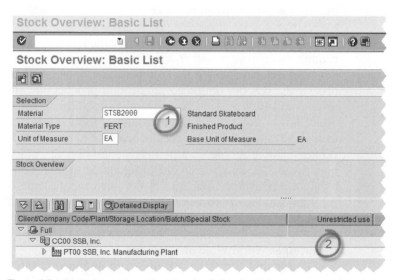

Figure 6.3 Inventory report for standard skateboards

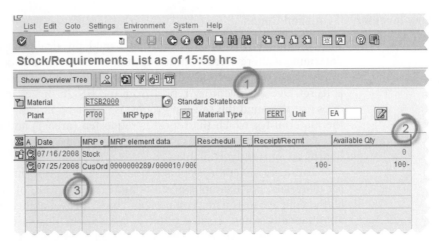

Figure 6.4   Stock requirement list skateboards—with sales order
Source: Copyright SAP AG 2008

Chapter 5, David (warehouse) requested production via a planned order when his periodic review of inventory indicated that more finished goods were needed. In our current example, Tim (warehouse) initiates production because he is the one who reviewed either the inventory report or the stock requirements list and realized that SSB had to produce skateboards to fill the specific customer order.

Alternatively, Matt (sales) can initiate production when he creates the sales order and performs a material availability check. He also has access to the stock requirements list. Remember that information about the process is available to anyone who is associated with the process and has access to the ES. If Matt is charged with the responsibility to ensure that sufficient inventory exists, then he creates the planned order when the sales order is generated. Under this system the process begins sooner than it would if Tim created the order after he received the inventory report. Going further, as we saw in previous chapters, in highly automated environments the ES can be configured to automatically review inventory and, if necessary, create the planned order. In all of these cases the ES helps SSB to complete the process steps faster.

Regardless of who creates the planned order, it must be reviewed by the production controller, and production must be authorized via a production order. In SSB, Catherine (production) has this responsibility. After reviewing all the planned orders, she has the option to create one production order for all the requested production or to consolidate several orders into a single production run. Very often, however, it is more beneficial to produce goods in fixed order quantities to take advantage of economies of scale or to deal with limitations of production capacity. For example, if SSB determines that the most economical production quantity is 200 skateboards but the planned orders total only 150, then SSB will create a production order for 200. In our example only one planned order exists for 100 skateboards to meet the customer order. We will assume that the most economical production quantity, also know as the **production lot size**, is 250. In this case, Catherine will authorize the production of 250 standard skateboards, despite the fact that World Wide ordered only 100.

Recall that the stock requirements list incorporates additional information as the various steps in the process are completed. Thus, at any time the stock

Figure 6.5A Stock requirements list skateboards—with planned order
Source: Copyright SAP AG 2008

Figure 6.5B Stock requirements list skateboards—with production order
Source: Copyright SAP AG 2008

requirements list provides information about the state of the process. Figures 6.5A and 6.5B show the stock requirements list after the planned order and production orders are created. In Figure 6.5A, the planned order (PldOrd in area 1) is displayed for 100 skateboards (area 2). In Figure 6.5B, however, the production order (PrdOrd in area 1) is for 250 skateboards (area 2), which is the production lot size.

In the production process discussed in Chapter 5, the next step is to issue raw materials to the production order. Again, in Chapter 5 we assumed that the raw materials are available. In this integrated example, we must first verify their availability. Therefore, a decision point is needed to verify that SSB has sufficient raw materials in house to complete the production order.

6.2.4 Review Inventory of Raw Materials

As with finished goods, several methods are available to assess the inventory of raw materials. In the procurement process discussed in Chapter 3, David (warehouse) physically observes that the inventory of raw materials is low, and he initiates the procurement process. In our example, Charlie (production) goes to the warehouse to obtain the necessary raw materials to begin producing the 250 skateboards. In the warehouse, Tim (warehouse) logs into the ES and retrieves an inventory report of all the materials needed to manufacture the skateboards. Alternatively, he retrieves a stock requirements list for these materials. Figure 6.6 shows an inventory report for the eight materials needed to make the standard skateboards. (Refer to the bill of materials in Chapter 5 for the quantity of each material that is needed to make one skateboard.) The inventory report confirms that there are sufficient quantities of all the necessary materials except the truck assembly (STTA2100, area 1). The report indicates that only 100 truck assemblies are available, whereas 500 are needed to make 250 skateboards. (Again, refer to the bill of materials in Chapter 5.) In response, Tim creates a purchase requisition to acquire 400 truck assemblies, and he initiates the procurement process.

There are several other strategies for initiating the procurement process. In one scenario, before Charlie goes to the warehouse, he retrieves an inventory report, observes the shortage of truck assemblies, and initiates the procurement process by creating a purchase requisition. In another scenario, Catherine reviews the inventory while authorizing production orders and creates the purchase requisition. In highly automated processes, the ES is configured to review inventory periodically

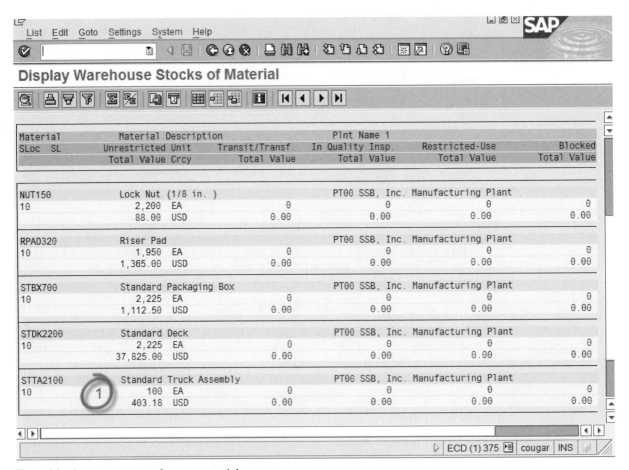

Figure 6.6 Inventory report for raw materials
Source: Copyright SAP AG 2008

and create purchase requisitions as needed. In each of these cases, the ES helps SSB to initiate procurement a little earlier than in the original scenario (where David initiates procurement) and to execute the process more quickly.

6.2.5 The Procurement Process

After the purchase requisition is created, the procurement process proceeds largely as described in Chapter 3. A purchase order is created and sent to a suitable vendor, goods are received into inventory, an invoice is received, and payment is made. In our example, we will assume that 1,000 standard truck assemblies are procured and received into inventory because the supplier offered a discount for purchasing this quantity. Once the raw materials are received into inventory, the subsequent steps associated with the procurement process (Receive Invoice, Send Payment) can be completed in parallel. This process is depicted in Figure 6.1, which depicts a path from the "receive shipment" step back to the "sufficient raw materials?" decision point.

Figures 6.7A–C show the stock requirements list for the truck assemblies as the steps in the procurement process progress. Figure 6.7A shows that 100 truck assemblies are in stock (area 1), a purchase requisition (PurRqs) for 400 truck assemblies has been created (area 2), and 500 truck assemblies are reserved for a production order (OrdRes in area 3). Figure 6.7B shows the same list after the requisition has been converted to a purchase order (POItem in area 1). Finally, Figure 6.7C shows the list after the materials have been received. Note that the inventory is now 1,100 (area 1).

Once the shipment from the vendor is received into the warehouse, an inventory report will reveal that 1,100 truck assemblies are available, and the production process can be resumed.

6.2.6 The Production Process Resumed

After SSB resumes production, the company must decide who should check the status of the inventory, and when. Again, several scenarios are possible. In our example, as described earlier, after Tim (warehouse) checks the inventory, he informs Charlie (production) that he cannot issue the needed materials. It is then Charlie's

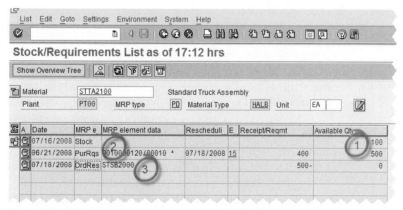

Figure 6.7A   Stock requirements list for truck assembly—after purchase requisition is created
Source: Copyright SAP AG 2008

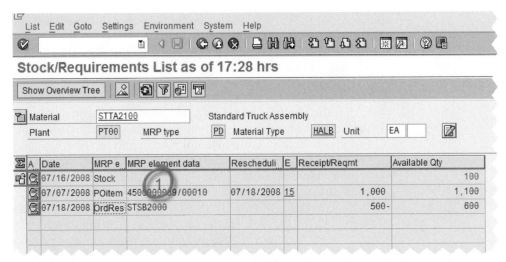

Figure 6.7B Stock requirements list for truck assembly—after purchase order is created
Source: Copyright SAP AG 2008

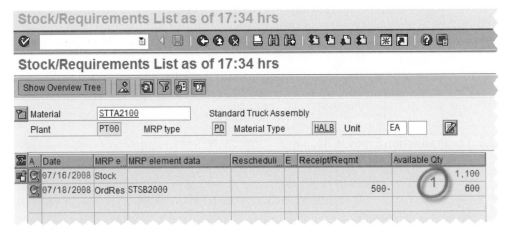

Figure 6.7C Stock requirements list for truck assembly—after goods receipt
Source: Copyright SAP AG 2008

responsibility to check inventory periodically (perhaps each morning). When he observes that a new shipment has been received, he returns to the warehouse to obtain the needed materials. Once he does this, the production process continues until the finished goods are received in the warehouse.

Alternatively, Tim can periodically check inventory and notify Charlie that he can now access the raw materials he needs to continue the production process. Finally, in highly automated processes, the ES can be configured to notify the appropriate persons when the needed materials are available.

Figure 6.8 shows an updated stock requirements list for the skateboards once the production process is resumed and completed. The planned order and production order shown in Figure 6.5 have disappeared, and there are now 250 skateboards in stock (area 1). Note that the customer order is still displayed, indicating that it has not been filled.

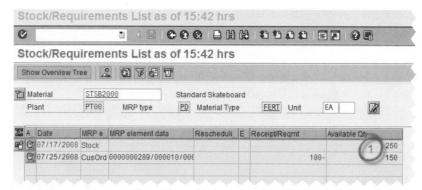

Figure 6.8 Stock requirements list for skateboard—after production
Source: Copyright SAP AG 2008

6.2.7 The Fulfillment Process Resumed

Once the production process has been completed and the skateboards are in finished goods inventory, the integrated process (Figure 6.1) returns to the decision point labeled "sufficient finished goods?" At this point, the fulfillment process can continue because there is now a sufficient inventory of completed skateboards to fulfill the customer order. Once again, the question arises as to who will check inventory of skateboards, and when. In our example, Tim (warehouse) will retrieve the delivery due list, as he does each morning, and check to see whether the materials in the orders due for delivery are available. When he checks the status of the order of 100 skateboards for World Wide, this time he finds that they are available. At this point, the fulfillment process continues (see Figure 6.1). When SSB receives payment for the 100 skateboards, the integrated process ends.

Figures 6.9A and 6.9B show the final stock requirements lists. Figure 6.9A shows that a delivery is in process (delivery in area 1). Figure 6.9B shows the status after the order has been shipped. The sales order is no longer listed, and the inventory drops to 150 skateboards (250 that were produced less the 100 that were shipped).

Figure 6.9A Stock requirements list for skateboard—during delivery
Source: Copyright SAP AG 2008

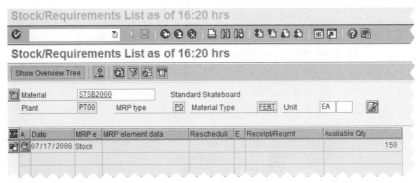

Figure 6.9B Stock requirements list for skateboard—after delivery
Source: Copyright SAP AG 2008

Hopefully, it is now clear to you that the three basic processes are really part of one larger integrated process. Once again, we have kept the processes deliberately simple, given the introductory nature of this book. In reality these processes are far more complex and can vary significantly from company to company.

In addition to procurement, fulfillment, and production there are many other intracompany and intercompany business processes. These processes involve people, equipment, and money. In the next section we examine some of these processes very briefly.

▶ 6.3 ADDITIONAL INTRACOMPANY PROCESSES

Two other core processes that exist in most companies are **human capital management (HCM)** and **asset management**. As the name suggests, HCM, which is also known as the **hire-to-retire** process, is concerned with people. Asset management, or the **acquire-to-retire** process, is concerned with physical assets such as machinery and computers. Let's take a closer look at both processes.

6.3.1 Human Capital Management

Human capital management is depicted in Figure 6.10. This process involves all the activities related to the recruitment of new employees, the management of those employees' careers while they are working at the company, and the eventual loss of those employees from the workforce due to either retirement or termination (voluntary or forced). Some of the steps in the hire-to-retire process contain very detailed subprocesses, such as recruitment, on-boarding (transitioning new employees into the company), career planning, performance management, and off-boarding (transitioning employees out of the company).

Figure 6.10 Human capital management process

Figure 6.11   Asset management process

6.3.2 Asset Management

Just as companies acquire raw materials, trading goods, and new employees, they also must acquire, maintain, and eventually dispose of assets such as machinery, computers, office furniture, and transportation equipment. Asset management, highlighted in Figure 6.11, includes activities related to procuring assets, maintaining and repairing assets, replacing assets, accounting for the depreciation of assets, and eventually disposing of, replacing, or retiring assets.

► 6.4 EXTENDED (INTERCOMPANY) PROCESSES

In Chapter 2 we briefly discussed the activities related to **supply chain management (SCM)**, **supplier relationship management (SRM)**, **product life cycle management (PLM)**, and **customer relationship management (CRM)** from an ES perspective. Refer back to Figures 2.5, 2.6, 2.7, and 2.8 to see how a typical ES system can help a company perform these processes more efficiently and profitably. In this section we briefly describe each of these processes. It is important to note that the name of the ES (e.g., SCM) has generally become synonymous with the business processes that it enables. In contrast, ERP is a generic term for an ES that enables multiple intracompany processes.

6.4.1 Supply Chain Management (SCM)

Most SCM systems are concerned with material planning and logistics (Figure 6.12). This process involves very complex planning to match the predicted demand for finished goods with both the production capacity and the raw materials requirements needed to meet that demand. SCM uses demand forecasts from the marketing and sales departments to create a demand plan for a specified period of time. It then matches that demand with the future production capacity available to the company to determine whether the company can produce the planned quantity of finished goods in the time required. After SCM generates this capacity plan, it creates a material plan to match the expected amount of finished goods to be produced with the amount of materials needed and the availability of those materials from the company's suppliers.

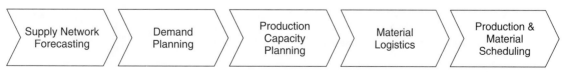

Figure 6.12   Plan-to-produce process in SCM

Figure 6.13 Source-to-settle process in SRM

Once the SCM system has determined how many finished goods are needed, how many goods the company can produce, and what raw materials the company requires, the company can then transfer those requirements to other systems for execution. For example, it can transfer the raw materials requirements to the SRM system (discussed next) to be matched against existing supplier contracts, supplier selection, and delivery schedules.

6.4.2 Supplier Relationship Management (SRM)

SRM systems enable the **source-to-settle** process (Figure 6.13) that occurs between a company and its suppliers. Although the simplified procurement process we discussed in this book involves working with a supplier, procurement is typically focused on the execution of the purchase order. In contrast, SRM focuses on the entire relationship between a company and its suppliers. This focus includes the purchasing process, but it also involves analyzing potential and existing suppliers, establishing purchasing contracts and ensuring compliance for purchasing against contracts, analyzing and managing all product purchases, requesting quotations and bids for complex products, and procuring office supplies and other nonproduction materials.

6.4.3 Product Life Cycle Management (PLM)

PLM systems enable the **idea-to-market** process (Figure 6.14), which interacts with many other processes in the company, such as SCM and SRM. In most organizations, products are the most vital assets. Not surprisingly, then, ensuring that the best ideas from inside and outside the company are converted to successful end products in the quickest and most economical way is a primary concern. PLM helps companies create a funnel of ideas that they can assess to determine the most viable end products for development. PLM also helps organizations to collaborate internally and externally to develop those products, to prepare their marketing and sales teams to sell those products, and to manage the quality of the products along the entire process. As we saw in the Procter and Gamble example earlier in the chapter, the management of new product ideas is critical for fast and affordable product innovation. The PLM process typically generates a large volume of documents. Therefore, most PLM solutions incorporate document and knowledge management capabilities so that everyone in the process has access to all of the historical background of the product.

Figure 6.14 Idea-to-market process in PLM

Figure 6.15 Demand-to-order process in CRM

6.4.4 Customer Relationship Management (CRM)

CRM systems extend the standard fulfillment process to incorporate a great deal of the activities that are involved with the **demand-to-order** processes (Figure 6.15). Demand-to-order consists of activities that (1) create demand for products through marketing campaigns, (2) transform that demand into sales opportunities, and (3) convert those sales opportunities into sales quotations and, ultimately, into sales orders. In addition, companies use CRM to manage the services they provide to customers after the sale to ensure that all product issues are quickly addressed and the customer relationship is kept strong. In essence, companies use CRM capabilities to build a wide base of interest for their products and to ensure that the money and effort they invest in marketing their products result in a high number of sales.

▶ 6.5 EXERCISE USING SIMULATED SAP ERP

Once again, it is now time for you to experience an enterprise system in action using a simulated SAP ERP environment.

Go to WileyPLUS and complete the exercises for this chapter. The exercise for this chapter consists of two parts, an exercise to execute the integrated process and a short quiz. Since you have completed all of the steps of the integrated process in earlier chapters, there will not be a guided exercise. It will be helpful if you review the exercises from Chapters 2, 3, 4 and 5 before starting the exercise for Chapter 6 to ensure that you recall the steps from the individual processes.

The excercise will take you through the following steps that have been discussed in this chapter:

1. Receive a customer inquiry
2. Create a quotation
3. Receive a customer purchase order
4. Create a sales order
5. Review the inventory of finished goods
6. Create a planned order
7. Convert the planned order to a production order
8. Review the inventory of raw materials
9. Create a purchase requisition for a number of raw materials
10. Convert the requisition to a purchase order
11. Receive goods from the vendor
12. Enter a vendor invoice into the system
13. Record a payment to the vendor
14. Review the inventory of raw materials (return to step 8, but this time follow a different path in the process)

15. Issue materials to the production order
16. Confirm the production of the finished goods
17. Move the finished materials to inventory
18. Review the inventory of finished goods (return to step 5, but this time follow a different path in the process)
19. Prepare the shipment (pick and pack)
20. Send the shipment (post goods issue)
21. Create a customer invoice
22. Receive a customer payment

After you complete the exercise, you will take a short quiz to test your knowledge of the integrated process. Your instructor will direct you to the location of the quiz. After you have completed the quiz, the system will grade it and send your score to your professor's grade book. You may view your score in the gradebook tab of WileyPLUS.

As before, please pay attention to what you are doing, and understand why the actions are necessary to execute the process. You may repeat these exercises as often as necessary to thoroughly understand the integrated nature of business processes and how an ES supports the integrated process.

▶ CHAPTER SUMMARY

In this chapter we have tied together the key processes of procurement, fulfillment, and production into an integrated process. Although previous chapters dealt with each key process independently and made assumptions about the availability of materials, the integrated process introduced the concepts of availability checks and decision points to illustrate the interdependencies among the key processes. Through this example, you saw how each process relies on the inputs and outputs of the other processes to function properly. This example also provided dramatic illustrations of the robust capabilities that an integrated ES can provide to employees throughout the execution of an integrated process.

The chapter also introduced some additional intra-company and intercompany processes that typically accompany procurement, fulfillment, and production. We explored the concept of assets through the discussion of human resource management and physical asset management. We also discussed extended processes that span the boundaries between and among companies.

At this point, you should have a clear understanding of both the key and the ancillary business processes that exist in the real world. Throughout this book, we have tried to simplify what are, in reality, very complex activities that you will encounter when you begin your career in business. With this basic knowledge of business processes, you will be very well prepared to adapt and adjust to the specific processes and operations of the organizations for which you will work. In addition, you will have a much deeper appreciation for the intricacies and dependencies between your tasks and the other areas of the organization.

▶ KEY TERMS

acquire-to-retire
asset management
availability check
customer relationship
    management (CRM)
decision point

demand-to-order
fixed order quantities
hire-to-retire
human capital
    management (HCM)
idea-to-market

integrated process
intercompany processes
intracompany processes
production lot size
product life cycle
    management (PLM)

source-to-settle
supplier relationship
    management (SRM)
supply chain
    management (SCM)

▶ REVIEW QUESTIONS

1. Identify and explain the key steps that integrate the procurement, fulfillment, and procurement processes.

2. The integrated process requires a company to suspend one process and branch out to another process, and then return to the previous process. How do the people involved in these processes know when to resume a process that was suspended?

3. Describe the objectives and key steps in the following processes.

    (a) Human capital management

    (b) Asset management

    (c) Product development

4. Explain the role of the following ES and how they "extend" the capabilities of the core processes that they support.

    (a) Supply chain management

    (b) Supplier relationship management

    (c) Product life cycle management

    (d) Customer relationship management

▶ ASSIGNMENTS

1. Select one ES from those discussed in this book (ERP, SCM, SRM, CRM, PLM), and provide examples of how companies are using these systems to improve their operations. Be specific about the benefits of using these systems.

2. Business network transformation (BNT) is an emerging concept whereby organizations depend on a network of partner organizations to transform their practices. Research this concept, and provide some examples of BNT achieved by organizations. Identify the various organizations that are part of the network. Explain how the work of these organizations has changed and how these changes have benefited the organization.

Appendix

List of Annotated Documents

- ▶ Goods Receipt Document
- ▶ Material Withdrawal Slip
- ▶ Packing List
- ▶ Picking Document
- ▶ Planned Order
- ▶ Production Order
- ▶ Purchase Order
- ▶ Purchase Requisition
- ▶ Quotation
- ▶ Sales Order
- ▶ Vendor Invoice

▶ Goods Receipt Document

Super Skateboard Builder, Inc
Goods Receipt Document
(Receipt Verification)

(1)

(2) **Receipt #** ___32343___

(3) **Receipt Date**	(4) **PO Number**	(5) **Vendor Number**	(6) **Vendor Name**
July 16, 2008	1546	43	Black Widow Skateboards

(7) Material #	(8) Description	(9) Unit Type	(10) Quantity Ordered	(11) Quantity Received	(12) Backorder Quantity
ENSB3000	Entry-Level Skateboard	Each	50	50	0
HLMT5000	Helmet	Each	10	10	0
SHRT4000	T-Shirt	Each	10	10	0
FAID6000	Skateboard First-aid Kits	Each	20	20	0

(13)

Received by:	Signature
Tim Jones	

Data in a goods receipt document:

	Field Name	Description
1.	Company Name	Name of the company receiving the goods
2.	Goods Receipt Number	A unique number identifying the document
3.	Receipt Date	Date that the goods were received
4.	PO Number	A unique number identifying the purchase order for which the goods are received
5.	Vendor Number	A unique number identifying the vendor
6.	Vendor Name	Name of the vendor that sent the shipment
7.	Material #	A unique number identifying the material
8.	Description	Description of the material
9.	Unit Type	The unit of measurement used to count the material. Examples include ounces, gallons, each, dozen, carton
10.	Quantity Ordered	Quantity of materials ordered
11.	Quantity Received	Quantity of materials received
12.	Backorder Quantity	Remaining goods to be delivered from original order
13.	Received By	The signature of the person receiving the materials

▶ Material Withdrawal Slip

Super Skateboard Builders, Inc. ① **Production Order #:** _4142_

Material Withdrawal Slip ② **Production Quantity:** _50_

③ Date	④ Issued by	⑤ Received by	⑥ Location	
7/23	TJ	CS	Warhouse	

⑦ Material Number	⑧ Material Description	⑨ Quantity per Skateboard	⑩ Total Quantity Needed	⑪ Quantity Issued
NUT 150	Lock Nut	8	400	400
BOLT 100	Bolt	8	400	400
STBX700	Packaging Box	1	50	50
LBL600	SSB Label	1	50	50
GTP600	Grip Tape	1	50	50
RPAD320	Riser Pads	2	100	100
STDK2200	Standard Deck	1	50	50
STTA2100	Standard Truck Assembly	2	100	100

Data in a material withdrawal slip:

	Field Name	Description
1.	Production Order #	The production order number
2.	Production Quantity	Number of units produced
3.	Date	Date of the Material Withdrawal Slip
4.	Issued By	The initials of the person who issued the materials
5.	Received By	The initials of the person who received the materials
6.	Location	Location of the material withdrawal
7.	Material Number	Number of the material issued
8.	Material Description	Description of the material issued
9.	Quantity per Skateboard	Quantity of raw materials needed to produce one skateboard
10.	Total Quantity Needed	Total quantity of raw materials to produce all the needed skateboards
11.	Quantity Issued	Quantity issued for production

▶ Packing List

Black Widow Skateboards, Inc.

1 Spider Way
Holland, MI, 49424 ①
Phone: 616.555.7834
Fax: 616.555.2387

Packing List

②	③	④	⑤	⑥
Order Date	**Customer Contact**	**Customer Number**	**Customer PO #**	**Order Number**
July 9, 2007	D. Bloomburg	4302	74052	29837
Date Filled ⑦	**Packed by**	**Checked by**	**Ship Date** ⑩	**Sales Rep** ⑪ **Shipped Via**
July 20, 2007	Jones ⑧	Smith ⑨	July 23, 2007	UPS Ground ⑫

Ship To:

Super Skateboard Builders, Inc.
1 Skateboard Drive
Grand Rapids, MI, 49525 ⑬

Bill To:

Super Skateboard Builders, Inc.
  Attention: David Bloomburg ⑭
1 Skateboard Drive
Grand Rapids, MI, 49525

⑮ Material #	⑯ Description	⑰ Unit Weight (lb)	⑱ Unit Type	⑲ Order Quantity	⑳ Ship Quantity	㉑ Backorder Quantity	㉒ Weight (lb)
ENSB3000	Entry-Level Skateboard	7.50	Each	50	50	0	375.00
HLMT5000	Helmet	4.00	Each	10	10	0	40.00
SHRT4000	T-Shirt	0.75	Each	10	10	0	7.50
FAID6000	Skateboard First-aid Kits	2.00	Each	20	20	0	40.00
							㉓
						Total Shipment Weight	462.50

Comments: Backordered items will ship as they become available.

㉔ **Please contact the Customer Service department at (616) 555-7834 with any questions or concerns.**

Thank you for your order!

Data in a packing list:

	Field Name	Description
1.	Sender Name and Address	Information about the company that sent the shipment
2.	Order Date	Date of the Purchase Order
3.	Customer Contact	Contact person in the customer's organization
4.	Customer Number	An unique number identifying the customer
5.	Customer PO Number	PO number in the customer's PO
6.	Order Number	Unique number identifying the order in the vendor's records
7.	Date Filled	The date the shipment was prepared
8.	Packed By	The name of the person preparing the shipment
9.	Checked By	The name of the person verifying the shipment
10.	Ship Date	The date the order was shipped
11.	Sales Rep	The name of the person taking the customer order
12.	Shipped Via	The method of shipment (e.g., ground, air) and the name of the transportation company (e.g., UPS, FedEx)
13.	Ship To	The address to which the shipment is to be sent
14.	Bill To	The address to which the invoice is to be sent
15.	Material Number	The material number(s) of the items in the shipment
16.	Description	The description of the materials in the shipment
17.	Unit Weight	The weight of one unit of each material in the shipment
18.	Unit Type	The unit of measurement used to count the material. Examples include ounces, gallons, each, dozen, carton
19.	Order Quantity	The quantity ordered
20.	Ship Quantity	The actual quantity shipped
21.	Backorder Quantity	The quantity to be shipped later, if the ship quantity is less than the order quantity
22.	Weight	The weight of the total number of units on each line
23.	Total Shipment Weight	The total weight of the shipment
24.	Notes	Any notes or special instructions

▶ Picking Document

Super Skateboard Builders, Inc. ①   **Picking Document**
1 Skateboard Drive
Grand Rapids, MI, 49525

BILL TO: **SHIP TO:**
World Wide Skateboard Distributors   World Wide Skateboard Distributors ③
Attention: P. Wilson   Mid West Warehouse
1229 Westwinde Street ②   1229 Westwinde Street
An Arbor, MI, 48109   An Arbor, MI, 48109
Phone 734.555.5638 Fax 734.555.55648   Phone 734.555.5638 Fax 734.555.55648

④ Order #	⑤ Customer PO #	⑥ P.O. DATE	⑦ Requested Delivery Date	⑧ SHIPPED VIA	⑨ F.O.B. POINT	⑩ TERMS
34567	100074	July 15, 2007	August 1, 2007	Ground	Destination	Net 30

Table 1 ⑪   ⑫   ⑬   ⑭   ⑮   ⑯

Material #	Material Description	Unit Type	Quantity Ordered	Storage Location	Quantity Picked	Storage Location
ENSB3000	Entry-Level Skateboard	Each	50	30	50	30
HLMT5000	Helmet	Each	10	30	10	30
SHRT4000	T-Shirt	Each	10	30	10	30
FAID6000	Skateboard First-aid Kits	Each	20	30	20	30

⑰ Picked by: _T. Jmns._   Date: **7/23/08**

Data in a picking document:

	Field Name	Description
1.	Sender's Name and Address	Information about the company that is filling the order
2.	Bill To	The address to which the invoice is being sent
3.	Ship To	The address to which the shipment was sent
4.	Order Number	The sales order number for which the material is being picked
5.	Customer PO Number	The number on the customer purchase order
6.	PO Date	The date the customer purchase order was created
7.	Requested Delivery Date	The date by which delivery of material is requested
8.	Shipped Via	The shipment method to be used. Options include ground, air, and rail
9.	FOB Point	Free on board point. The point at which ownership of goods passes from the sender to the recipient. Typical values are shipping point and receiving point or destination
10.	Terms	Terms of payment
11.	Material Number	The number identifying the material picked
12.	Material Description	A description of the material picked
13.	Unit Type	The unit of measurement used to count the material. Examples include ounces, gallons, each, dozen, carton
14.	Quantity Ordered	The quantities of the materials ordered
15.	Quantity Picked	The quantities of the materials picked
16.	Storage Location	The location in the warehouse from where the material was picked
17.	Picked By	The name of the person completing the picking task and the date the picking was completed

▶ Planned Order

Super Skateboard Builders, Inc.	① Planned Order #: 7412
Planned Order	② Production Order #: 4142
	(to be filled in by Production Controller)

③ Request Date	④ Requested Delivery Date	⑤ Requester Name	⑥ Requester Phone	⑦ Delivery Location
7/9/07	7/22/07	Bloomburg	555-1234	Warehouse

⑧ Material Number	⑨ Material Description	⑩ Quantity
STSB 2000	Std. Skateboard	50

Requested by: _David Bloomburg_   Date: 7/9/07
⑪

Approved by: _C. Vanduboss._   Date: 7/10/07
⑫

Data in a production order:

	Field Name	Description
1.	Production Order Number	A unique number identifying the order. This number is used to track the status of the order
2.	Material Number	Number of the material to be produced
3.	Material Description	Description of the material to be produced
4.	Quantity	The quantity of the material being ordered
5.	Date	Date the specified steps were completed
6.	Quantity Complete	Quantity completed for the specified steps
7.	Scrap Quantity	Scrap quantity for the specified steps
8.	Completed By	Initials of the person completing the step
9.	Planned Order Number	The planned order for which production is being completed
10.	Authorized By	The signature of the person authorizing the production order
11.	Date Authorized	Date of authorization

▶ Purchase Order

Super Skateboard Builders, Inc.

1 Skateboard Drive ①
Grand Rapids, MI, 49525
Phone: 616.555.1234 Fax: 616.555.2234

PURCHASE ORDER
Purchase Order Number: 74052
②

THE PURCHASE ORDER NUMBER MUST APPEAR ON ALL RELATED CORRESPONDENCE, SHIPPING PAPERS, AND INVOICES
③

TO:
Black Widow Skateboards, Inc ④
1 Spider Way
Holland, MI, 49424
616.555.7834

SHIP TO:
Mr. David Bloomburg ⑤
SSB, Inc.
1 Skateboard Drive
Grand Rapids, MI, 49525
616.555.1234

⑥ Purchase Order #	⑦ P.O. DATE	⑧ Delivery Date	⑨ Shipped VIA	⑩ F.O.B. Point	⑪ Payment Terms
74052	July 9, 2007	July 27, 2007	Ground	Receiving Dock	Net 30

⑫ Quantity	⑬ Material #	⑭ Material Description	⑮ Unit Type	⑯ Unit Price	⑰ Item Total
50	ENSB3000	Entry-Level Skateboard	Each	34.00	1,700.00
10	HLMT5000	Helmet	Each	20.00	200.00
10	SHRT4000	T-Shirt	Each	7.00	70.00
20	FAID6000	Skateboard First-aid Kits	Each	10.00	200.00

⑱	SUBTOTAL	$ 2,170.00
⑲	SALES TAX	Exempt
⑳	SHIPPING & HANDLING	Included
㉑	OTHER	N/A
㉒	ORDER TOTAL	$ 2,170.00

Authorized by: _____
M. Seward, Purchasing Manager
㉓

Date 7/18/07
㉔

Data in a purchase order:

	Field Name	Description
1.	Company Name and Address	
2.	Purchase Order Number	A unique number identifying the order. This number is used to track the status of the order
3.	Notices	Any special notices to the vendor regarding the order
4.	Vendor Information	The name and address of the vendor to whom the purchase order will be sent
5.	Receiver Information	The name and address of the company to whom the shipment is to be sent
6.	Purchase Order Number	Often the PO number is printed in more than one location
7.	PO Date	The date the purchase order was created
8.	Delivery Date	The requested delivery date for the shipment
9.	Shipment Via	The shipment method to be used. Options include ground, air, and rail
10.	FOB Point	Free on Board point. The point at which ownership of goods passes from the sender to the recipient. Typical values are shipping point and receiving point or destination
11.	Payment Terms	Terms of payment
12.	Quantity	The quantities of the material being ordered
13.	Material Number	Material number
14.	Material Description	Material description
15.	Unit Type	The unit of measurement used to count the material. Examples include ounces, gallons, each, dozen, carton
16.	Unit Price	The cost of one unit of the material
17.	Item Total	The total cost of the material on each line of the order. This is the unit price multiplied by the order quantity
18.	Subtotal	This is a total of all the line items
19.	Sales Tax	Any applicable sales taxes
20.	Shipping and Handling	Cost of shipping and handling
21.	Other	Other charges, such as those associated with special orders or rush orders
22.	Order Total	The grand total of the order and is the sum of the subtotal, sales tax, shipping and handling, and other charges
23.	Signature	The signature of the person authorizing the purchase order
24.	Date	The date the order was signed

► Purchase Requisition

① Super Skateboard Builders, Inc.
Purchase Requisition ② **Requisition Number**: _____3754_____
③ **PO Number**: _____1546_____
(to be filled in by Purchasing)

④ Request Date	⑤ Requested Delivery Date	⑥ Requester Name	⑦ Requester Extension	⑧ Delivery Location
7/9/07	7/27/07	D. Bloomburg	3984	Warehouse

⑨ Material #	⑩ Material Description	⑪ Quantity
ENSB3000	Entry-Level Skateboard	50
HLMT5000	Helmet	10
SHRT4000	T-Shirt	10
FAID6000	Skateboard First-aid Kits	20

For use by Purchasing					
PO Date	Vendor	Requested Date	Delivery Location	F.O.B. POINT	TERMS
7/11/07	Black Widow Skateboards, Inc.	July 27, 2007	Warehouse	Destination	Net 30
⑫	⑬	⑭	⑮	⑯	⑰

⑱ Requisitioned by:	Name D. Bloomburg	Signature	Date: 7/9/07
⑲ PO created by:	Name M. SEWARD	Signature	Date: 7/11/07

Data in a purchase requisition:

	Field Name	Description
1.	Sender's Name	Company information
2.	Requisition Number	A number uniquely identifying the requisition
3.	PO Number	A number uniquely identifying the PO
4.	Request Date	The date the requisition was created
5.	Requested Delivery Date	The requested delivery date for the shipment
6.	Requester Name	Name of individual requesting purchase
7.	Requester Extension	Contact info of requester
8.	Delivery Location	Location to deliver goods
9.	Material Number	Material number
10.	Material Description	Material description
11.	Quantity	The quantities of the material being requested
12.	PO Date	The date the purchase order was created
13.	Vendor	Name of the vendor to whom the PO is sent
14.	Requested Date	Delivery date requested in the PO
15.	Delivery Location	Delivery location requested in the PO
16.	F.O.B. Point	Free on board point. The point at which ownership of goods passes from the sender to the recipient. Typical values are shipping point and receiving point or destination
17.	Terms	Terms of Payment
18.	Requisitioned by	Data about the person who created the requisition
19.	PO created by	Data about the person who created the PO

▶ Quotation

Super Skateboard Builders, Inc.

1 Skateboard Drive, Grand Rapids, MI, 49525 ①
Phone 616.555.1234 Fax 616.555.1235

② # Quotation
Quotation Number: 1100435

TO: ③
Mr. Patrick Wilson
World Wide Skateboard Distributors
1229 Westwinde Street
Ann Arbor, MI, 48109

④ Date: 6/6/08
This quotation is valid for 30 days.
Terms of payment: Net 30
Terms of delivery: FOB Receiving Dock

⑤ Quantity	⑥ Material #	⑦ Material Description	⑧ Unit Type	⑨ Unit Price	⑩ Item Total
50	ENSB3000	Entry-Level Skateboard	Each	45.00	2,250.00
10	HLMT5000	Helmet	Each	27.00	270.00
10	SHRT4000	T-Shirt	Each	10.00	100.00
20	FAID6000	Skateboard First-aid Kits	Each	16.00	320.00

⑪ SUBTOTAL	$ 2,940.00
⑫ SALES TAX	Exempt
⑬ SHIPPING & HANDLING	Included
⑭ OTHER	N/A
⑮ ORDER TOTAL	$ 2,940.00

Authorized by: _M Jones_
Matt Jones, Sales Associate ⑯

Date
⑰ 6/6/08

Data in a quotation:

	Field Name	Description
1.	Company Name and Address	
2.	Quotation Number	A unique number identifying the quotation. This number is used to track the status of the quotation
3.	Who the quotation was sent to	The name and address of the person to whom the quotation was sent
4.	Terms of the Quotation	Examples of possible terms of the quotation are terms of delivery, terms of payment, and valid to date
5.	Quantity	The quantities of the material
6.	Material Number	The number identifying the material
7.	Material Description	A description of the material
8.	Unit Type	The unit of measurement used to count the material. Examples include ounces, gallons, each, dozen, carton
9.	Unit Price	The cost of one unit of the material
10.	Item Total	The total cost of the material on each line of the order. This is the unit price multiplied by the order quantity
11.	Subtotal	This is a total of all the line items
12.	Sales Tax	Any applicable sales taxes
13.	Shipping and Handling	Cost of shipping and handling
14.	Other	Other charges, such as those associated with special orders or rush orders
15.	Order Total	The grand total of the order and is the sum of the subtotal, sales tax, shipping and handling, and other charges
16.	Signature	The signature of the person authorizing the quotation
17.	Date	The date the quotation was signed

▶ Sales Order

Super Skateboard Builders, Inc. ①

Sales Order

BILL TO:
World Wide Skateboard Distributors
Attention: P. Wilson
1229 Westwinde Street ②
An Arbor, MI, 48109
Phone 734.555.5638 Fax 734.555.55648

SHIP TO:
World Wide Skateboard Distributors
Mid West Warehouse
1229 Westwinde Street ③
An Arbor, MI, 48109
Phone 734.555.5638 Fax 734.555.55648

④ ⑤ ⑥ ⑦ ⑧ ⑨ ⑩

Order #	Customer PO #	P.O. DATE	Requested Delivery Date	SHIPPED VIA	F.O.B. POINT	TERMS
34567	100074	July 15, 2008	August 1, 2007	Ground	Receiving Dock	Net 30

⑪ ⑫ ⑬ ⑭ ⑮ ⑯

Quantity	Material #	Material Description	Unit Type	Unit Price	Total
50	ENSB3000	Entry-Level Skateboard	Each	45.00	2,250.00
10	HLMT5000	Helmet	Each	27.00	270.00
10	SHRT4000	T-Shirt	Each	10.00	100.00
20	FAID6000	Skateboard First-aid Kits	Each	16.00	320.00

SUBTOTAL ⑰	$ 2,940.00
SALES TAX ⑱	Exempt
SHIPPING & HANDLING ⑲	Included
OTHER ⑳	N/A
TOTAL ㉑	$ 2,940.00

㉒ Received by: _M. Jones_ Date: _7/18/08_

㉓ Packed by: _T. Jms._ Date: _7/23/08_

㉔ Shipped by: _T. Jon_ Date: _7/24/08_

㉕ Invoiced by: _Shane Smith_ Date: _7/30/08_

㉖ Payment received by: _Shane Smith_ Date: _8/7/08_

Data in a sales order:

	Field Name	Description
1.	Company Name	Name of the company selling the products
2.	Bill To	Address to send the invoice
3.	Ship To	Address to send the shipment
4.	Order #	A unique number identifying the order. This number is used to track the status of the order
5.	Customer PO #	Customer's purchase order number
6.	P.O. Date	The date the purchase order was created
7.	Requested Delivery Date	Date delivery of materials is requested
8.	Shipped Via	The shipment method to be used. Options include ground, air, and rail
9.	F.O.B. Point	Free on board point. The point at which ownership of goods passes from the sender to the recipient. Typical values are shipping point and receiving point or destination
10.	Terms	Terms of payment
11.	Quantity	The quantities of the material being ordered
12.	Material #	Material number
13.	Material Description	Material description
14.	Unit Type	The unit of measurement used to count the material. Examples include ounces, gallons, each, dozen, carton
15.	Unit Price	The cost of one unit of the material
16.	Total	The total cost of the material on each line of the order. This is the unit price multiplied by the order quantity
17.	Subtotal	This is a total of all the line items
18.	Sales Tax	Any applicable sales taxes
19.	Shipping & Handling	Cost of shipping and handling
20.	Other	Other charges, such as those associated with special orders or rush orders
21.	Order Total	The grand total of the order and is the sum of the subtotal, sales tax, shipping and handling, and other charges
22.	Received By	The signature of the person receiving the order and the date the order was received
23.	Packed By	The signature of the person packing the order and the date the order was packed
24.	Shipped By	The signature of the person shipping the order and the date the order was shipped
25.	Invoiced By	The signature of the person invoicing the order and the date the order was invoiced
26.	Payment received By	The signature of the person receiving the payment for the order

▶ Vendor Invoice

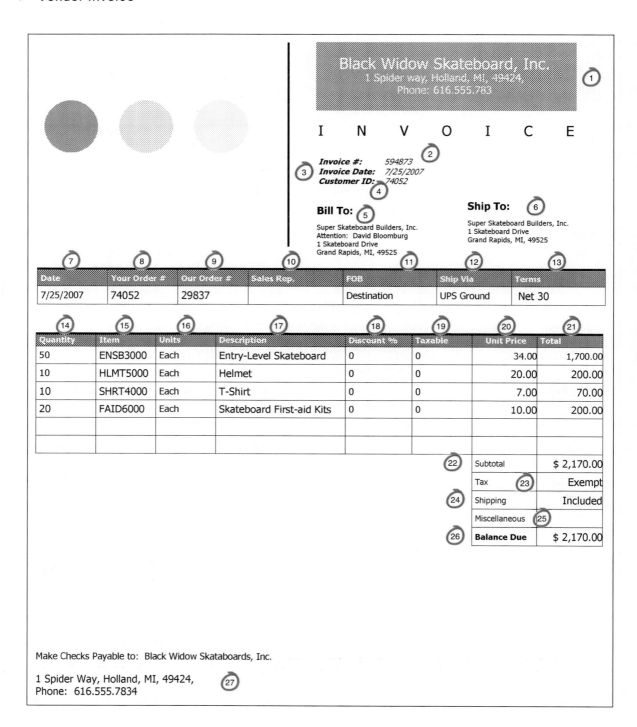

Black Widow Skateboard, Inc.
1 Spider way, Holland, MI, 49424,
Phone: 616.555.783

I N V O I C E

Invoice #: 594873
Invoice Date: 7/25/2007
Customer ID: 74052

Bill To:
Super Skateboard Builders, Inc.
Attention: David Bloomburg
1 Skateboard Drive
Grand Rapids, MI, 49525

Ship To:
Super Skateboard Builders, Inc.
1 Skateboard Drive
Grand Rapids, MI, 49525

Date	Your Order #	Our Order #	Sales Rep.	FOB	Ship Via	Terms
7/25/2007	74052	29837		Destination	UPS Ground	Net 30

Quantity	Item	Units	Description	Discount %	Taxable	Unit Price	Total
50	ENSB3000	Each	Entry-Level Skateboard	0	0	34.00	1,700.00
10	HLMT5000	Each	Helmet	0	0	20.00	200.00
10	SHRT4000	Each	T-Shirt	0	0	7.00	70.00
20	FAID6000	Each	Skateboard First-aid Kits	0	0	10.00	200.00

Subtotal	$ 2,170.00
Tax	Exempt
Shipping	Included
Miscellaneous	
Balance Due	$ 2,170.00

Make Checks Payable to: Black Widow Skataboards, Inc.

1 Spider Way, Holland, MI, 49424,
Phone: 616.555.7834

Data in a vendor invoice:

	Field Name	Description
1.	Sender Name and Address	Information about the company that sent the invoice
2.	Invoice Number	A number uniquely identifying the invoice
3.	Invoice Date	Date the invoice was created
4.	Customer ID	A number that uniquely identifies the customer to the vendor
5.	Bill To	The address to which the invoice is being sent
6.	Ship To	The address to which the shipment was sent
7.	Invoice Date	Date the invoice was created
8.	Your Order Number	The customer purchase order number
9.	Our Order Number	The sales order number
10.	Sales Rep	The name of the salesperson who took the order
11.	FOB	Free on Board point. The point at which ownership of goods passes from the sender to the recipient. Typical values are shipping point and receiving point or destination
12.	Ship Via	The shipment method to be used. Options include ground, air, and rail. In addition a transportation company may be included
13.	Terms	Terms of payment
14.	Quantity	The number of units the invoice is for
15.	Items	The material that the invoice is for
16.	Units	The unit of measurement used to count the material. Examples include ounces, gallons, each, dozen, carton
17.	Description	The description of the material
18.	Discount %	The discount provided
19.	Taxable	The taxable amount of for each item in the invoice
20.	Unit Price	The price per unit for each material in the invoice
21.	Total	The total amount for each material in the invoice
22.	Subtotal	The sum of the amounts for each material in the invoice
23.	Tax	The amount of tax
24.	Shipping	Shipping and handling charges
25.	Miscellaneous	Other charges, such as those for special orders or expedited orders
26.	Balance Due	The total amount due
27.	Payment Address	The address to which payment should be sent

Index